IRENE

LYNNE C. SWANSON

CONTENTS

IRENE

LYNNE C. SWANSON

"BREAKING BARRIERS"

THE PIONEERING JOURNEY OF LANCASHIRE´S FIRST CID POLICEWOMAN

L C. SWANSON

Port Sunlight Village Lancashire

My first childhood memory was the war memorial in the village of Port Sunlight this quaint village nestled in the northwest of England, holds a unique allure with its idyllic setting and carefully crafted architecture.

Under the grand oak tree at the heart of the garden, my grandfather would often share stories about Ireland and we would indulge our favourite treats. Whether it was sharing ice cream cones on sunny afternoons or sipping hot cocoa on crisp winter days, every moment was a precious memory etched in my heart.

PHOTOGRAPHY BY
BRIAN SWANSON

Acknowledgements

I extend my heartfelt gratitude to my friends and family for their unwavering support throughout my journey of crafting this book. To John and Ben, Patricia, Jasmine, Martin, Shirley and Lorraine, thank you for your patience and willingness to bear with my numerous inquiries. I thank Brian Swanson for the beautiful Photography.

However, my deepest appreciation goes to those who dedicated their precious time to read my Novella and sharing in the captivating memories of Irene. Your encouragement and feedback have been invaluable.

Lastly, I wish to offer a token of assistance to aspiring writers embarking on their literary adventures. Below, you'll find links to helpful resources that I hope will prove beneficial in your book-writing endeavours.

Thank you all for being a part of this enriching experience.

With warm regards,

PROLOGUE

In this factual biography, I invite you to join me on a captivating journey as I share the remarkable life of Irene, a woman of courage and resilience. Our story begins in 2007 when I had the privilege of owning a beauty salon in the village of La Marina, Elche, Alicante, Spain, and first encountered Irene. Over a decade, Irene became a regular visitor to my salon, and our interactions grew into cherished moments of camaraderie and genuine friendship. Captivated by the incredible stories Irene shared during our pampering sessions, I sought her permission to write a biography about her life, promising to protect the identities of those involved, including Irene's. This is the untold story of Irene, an extraordinary woman whose life was filled with moments of inspiration and strength.

In the quaint village of La Marina, our paths converged - Irene, with her rich life experiences, and I, the owner of the beauty salon. From our first meeting, an inexplicable connection sparked, and Irene's frequent visits to my salon soon blossomed into much more than beauty sessions. As time passed, Irene gradually opened up and shared the profound stories of her life, tales of bravery and resilience.y, love, and resilience that left me captivated and in awe. Each pampering session turned into an opportunity to delve into her life's journey and the events that shaped her into the person she had become.

Enthralled by Irene's captivating narratives, I felt compelled to capture her life in a biography. Seeking her approval, I asked Irene for permission to write her story, promising to safeguard the identities of all involved, just as she wished.

In honouring Irene's request, I approached the task with great care, making sure to alter the names and identities of the individuals who played roles in Irene's life. Respecting her privacy, I aimed to tell her story while preserving the confidentiality of those she held dear.

Throughout the process of crafting Irene's biography, I felt privileged to have the chance to know her and to hear about her remarkable journey. Our interactions went beyond the traditional roles of salon owner and client, creating a bond that transcended the ordinary.

As Irene's biography began to take shape, it revealed a life adorned with courage, love, and resilience. Her journey was a testament to the strength of the human spirit, as she navigated life's challenges with grace and determination.

Writing Irene's biography filled me with immense gratitude for the opportunity to be part of her life. Sharing her story with the world felt like a privilege, as it allowed others to glimpse the beauty of human connections and the transformative power of shared experiences.

I have endeavoured to share the extraordinary life of Irene - a woman of courage and resilience who touched the hearts of those around her, including mine. Our journey together, filled with genuine friendship and captivating stories, is a testament to the power of human connections and the beauty that lies within each of us. As we travel through the journey of her life remains an enduring reminder that courage and strength can be found amidst life's challenges and triumphs, inspiring us to embrace our journeys with unwavering determination and hope.

CHAPTER ONE

REMINISCING THE WAR YEARS - LIFE AND NOSTALGIA IN 1930S ENGLAND

B orn amidst the turmoil of World War II in 1936, my early memories are woven with recollections of the German bombers soaring overhead, destined for the Barrow-in-Furness shipyard on the other side of Morecambe Bay. Those were the days of blackout curtains on windows, but my curiosity for reading resulted in my mother removing the bulb from my bedroom to discourage my nighttime escapades. I, however, managed to acquire a candle and some matches, attempting to continue my nocturnal reading, but my mother swiftly intervened.

The constant buzz of aircraft overhead was a reminder of the war's proximity, leaving me wondering if the planes would ever bomb near our home, as the distance to Barrow was only about 50 miles.

The presence of American troops passing through our area was a thrilling event. Word would spread among the neighbourhood kids when the American convoys were expected, and we would eagerly gather by the main A6 Road, hoping for some treats like gum and tins of Spam thrown by the passing soldiers. Despite my mother's cautious warnings, the Americans were kind and generous, and I occasionally returned home with a few tins to her disapproval.

Life during rationing times was surprisingly pleasant, with homegrown vegetables abundant in our gardens. My mother, a skilled cook, mastered the art of preparing delicious meals despite the limited supplies. We cherished simple lunches at school and modest dinners at home, savouring every morsel without waste.

In those days, the absence of plastic and minimal waste was the norm. People found innovative ways to repurpose things. My grandfather constructed a beautiful garden seat from branches he gathered in the woods.

Our family tended to hens in a spacious hen house, but a humorous incident occurred when we attempted to have roast chicken for Easter Sunday lunch. My father endeavoured to wring the chicken's neck (something he had never done before), the persistent chicken survived his amateurish attempts, and with its poor neck stretched my mother felt sorry for the chicken and made a splint bandaging it around its neck. Graciously it survived! Such experiences were common as most families were accustomed to raising and preparing their poultry.

Gardening was a tradition carried on by my grandparents. My parents planted various crops, including peas, radishes, tomatoes, and potatoes. Planting new potatoes by the light of a full moon was a folklore practice that our neighbours adhered to, and we joined them in eager anticipation of the event.

CHAPTER TWO

CHILDHOOD MEMORIES: PORT SUNLIGHT, TRANQUILLITY TO TRIALS AND TRIUMPHS

M y Grandparents resided in the village of Port Sunlight, the quaint and charming village nestled in the northwest of England, which holds a unique allure with its idyllic setting and carefully crafted architecture. One of the standout features of this village is Park Road, a picturesque avenue with its well-manicured gardens and tree-lined path. It had an exquisite ornamental stone bridge.

 The village had winding streets with benches which presented a peaceful oasis where residents and visitors alike could escape the hustle and bustle of daily life. The sight of the lush greenery, the gentle babbling of a nearby stream, and the subtle fragrance of blooming flowers created an atmosphere of serenity and tranquillity.

Port Sunlight had much to offer beyond its natural beauty. The Garden Village, as it was affectionately known, boasted an array of public amenities thoughtfully designed for the well-being and enjoyment of its residents.

 The commitment to the community's welfare was evident in the presence of a well-equipped hospital and schools, fostering an environment of growth and learning for the village's young residents. For moments of leisure and entertainment, a grand concert hall echoed with the harmonies of various performances, enriching the cultural tapestry of the village. On warmer days, the open-air swimming pool offered a refreshing escape, enticing families and friends to gather for joyous splashes and laughter. How I enjoyed many childhood visits to my grandparent's village and all the facilities it offered giving me unforgettable memories.

Nestled in the heart of the village was a poignant reminder of sacrifice and courage: the War Memorial. This revered monument stood as a solemn tribute to the valiant soldiers who made the ultimate sacrifice during World War One. Every year, my grandparents, parents and I joined the locals in a heartfelt tradition of paying our respects to these fallen heroes. The annual parade, a sombre yet poignant occasion, brought together the entire community to honour the memory of those who bravely faced the ravages of war.

One of my earliest childhood memories transports me to that village. It was during a memorial service, which was held every year. I was about 20 months old, comfortably seated in my pushchair when, all of a sudden, I found myself at the curb's edge. Unfortunately, the pram slid backwards, trapping my foot under the bar. The intense pain from that incident is still vivid in my memories. In a rush, my mother promptly took me to the hospital. Thankfully, despite ending up with bruises and swelling, there were no lasting injuries. I have so many happy memories, most notably her cherished visits to the gardens of the Bridge End Pub in the Port Sunlight. These visits were special because I spent time with my grandparents, with a particular emphasis on the deep bond I shared with my doting grandfather.

In the tranquil ambience of the pub's gardens, I would spend countless hours exploring the vibrant flora, listening to the soothing sound of birdsong, and looking at the wildlife, but what truly made these moments magical was the unwavering love and affection her grandfather bestowed upon me.

Under the grand oak tree at the heart of the garden, my grandfather would often share stories about Ireland and we would indulge our favourite treats. Whether it was sharing ice cream cones on sunny afternoons or sipping hot cocoa on crisp winter days, every moment was a precious memory etched in my heart.

Another memory from my childhood revolves around a teddy bear that remains in my possession to this day. My mother had gifted me the bear, but when I was around three or four years old, I decided to trim off all its fur. My mother was understandably furious. However, she went to the market, purchased some fur, and skillfully sewed it back onto the teddy bear. I cannot bear to part with that teddy; it still occupies a special place on my bed.

My memories also extend to my early school years. At infant school, they would put us in cots for a few hours during the day to sleep. I recall the soothing songs they would sing to us and the joy of creating drawings and pictures. These were truly happy memories from our time as young children. Transitioning to junior school, I distinctly remember pleading with my parents to allow me to have school dinners. The reason for my persistence was the exceptional cook at the school. She had a talent for preparing delicious pastries, and her meat and fish pies were especially delightful.

One particular memory from Sunday school stands out, but not for positive reasons. The vicar approached me one day and invited me to sit on his lap. Oblivious to any ill intentions, I obliged. However, when he patted my bottom and gave me an apple, I felt something was amiss. Upon returning home, my grandparents noticed my tardiness and inquired about it. I innocently mentioned that the vicar had given me a "rotten" apple. The look on their faces made it clear that something was wrong, though I hadn't fully grasped the situation. On another occasion, when the vicar visited our home, my grandfather took a stand. He confronted the vicar and wrapped his bike around the clergyman's neck, sending a strong message about his misconduct. He had sent me upstairs to my bedroom. I remember seeing the bike wrapped around the clergyman's neck and my grandfather shouting go and explain that to your parishioners!

During my senior school years, I encountered a different kind of influence as we were taught by nuns. One particular teacher, Miss Duffy, held fanatical beliefs. She propagated the notion that Catholics were the lost tribe of Israel and saw themselves as the chosen people. Appalled by her teachings, I shared this information with my grandmother, who lived with us at the time. The very next day, my grandmother went to the school and withdrew me from Miss Duffy's class. It was a time when children could easily be influenced and subjected to brainwashing, and my family took a stand against such fanaticism. These childhood memories, ranging from painful incidents to heartwarming moments and unsettling encounters, have shaped my understanding and resilience as I journey through life.

CHAPTER THREE

A JOURNEY OF ACHIEVEMENT'S AND CHALLENGES

I n my youth, I enjoyed playing rounders and tennis occasionally, but sports weren't my forte. My true passion lay in writing and English composition, making those my favourite subjects in school. At age 15, an opportunity arose when the Temperance Society came to our school, urging students to write about the drawbacks of drinking. I took up the challenge and meticulously penned my thoughts, earning myself a Certificate of Special Merit for my essay. As I grew older, my mother would humorously point out the irony of my advocating against drinking while enjoying a gin.

Exams, however, were a different story for me. I struggled with fear and anxiety whenever I had to face them, causing me to panic and even dismantle my watch on one occasion.

The fear of failure loomed over me, and it affected my performance. Though not explicitly critical, my mother would stay silent in response to my exam results, which I found more challenging to bear than any words.

One fond memory from my childhood was my white and red bike, which I adored. However, I recall receiving a slap one night when I arrived home late, explaining that I didn't have a watch to keep track of time. My mother responded that I had to guess, a reminder to be responsible for my actions.

Throughout my life, I faced triumphs and challenges, excelling in writing and English while confronting my fear of exams and the consequences of being late. Despite my mother's sternness, I understood that her intentions were well-meaning. This journey has been happy and sad with lessons learned along the way.

CHAPTER FOUR

MOTHERS STRUGGLE TO ACCEPT MY CHOICES

M y mother possessed a cautious nature, and my father worked as a baker, earning a steady income. When I decided to join the police force, I received a letter inviting me for an interview in Preston. My mother, unaware of my intentions, discovered the letter addressed to me saying I had got the job. She was furious, and I can vividly recall my mother waving the letter about, her disapproval evident and believing that I had pursued this opportunity solely to escape from home. I had to be honest, knowing that she was not the most affectionate parent. The police interview at our house made my mother and father quite nervous, leaving me worried that I would be trapped at home indefinitely.

It was a time when getting an education and then getting married and starting a family was the norm. However, I yearned for something more, wanting to make a difference in my life. Although she didn't physically harm me, her words cut deep, and I wished I had mustered the courage to claim ownership of the letter.

Emotions were seldom shown by my mother, and displays of affection were rare. I once pointed out to her that she had never given me a personal gift. My birthday was the week before Christmas, the occasions were always combined, and while she provided monetary gifts, they lacked personal thought or sentiment. Years later, when I turned 30, my mother surprised me with a small trinket box adorned with seashells. It was an atrocious item, but I still retain it somewhere, a token of her attempt at a personal gift.

At times, I felt like I didn't belong within my own family, entertaining thoughts that perhaps I had been adopted. he didn't resemble any of the family members in Ireland. The Irish tended to exhibit more warmth and affection, unlike my mother.

As I grew up, my mother often spoke of her education, revealing that the headmaster had recognized her intellectual potential and encouraged her to sit exams for university. However, my grandmother forbade it, and my mother never pursued her academic dreams. Despite this setback, she possessed a remarkable talent for writing beautiful poetry and capturing her thoughts in a diary-like notebook during our annual holidays. She harboured bitterness about her unfulfilled aspirations, though she may not have been consciously aware of it. It could have been a transformative experience for her. On one occasion, I expressed a desire to become a vet, to which she responded that people like us don't pursue such careers. It was a prevailing mindset of the 1950s, where ordinary individuals rarely ventured into professional fields requiring certifications. Today, talent is recognized and nurtured, regardless of background or social status.

Mother excelled in cooking, particularly on Wednesdays when she prepared sausages, Yorkshire puddings, stuffing, mushy peas, mashed potatoes, roasted potatoes, and onion gravy. One of my police officer friends, who worked in traffic control, would regularly visit our home on Wednesdays solely for the onion gravy, which she found exquisite. Today, one would typically purchase a kilogram of sausages, but my mother would only acquire half a pound. My father would have 3, and I had 2 sausages, while she, not being a big eater, had only one. The Yorkshire puddings she made were enormous, surpassing any culinary efforts of my grandmother, who was a terrible cook. When my grandfather returned home from work around 6 o'clock, my grandmother would hastily chop vegetables and place the meat in the oven, resulting in a tasteless meal. During my mother's hospitalization, my grandmother moved in to take care of me. My father would often remark, "Jesus, Mary, you can't cook!" displaying his dissatisfaction with her culinary skills.

On Fridays, my grandmother would cook Manx kippers, She used to heat a lump of lard into the frying pan on a high heat, and flames engulfed the kippers resulting in an unpleasant odour. My mother, however, had a natural knack for cooking, and on Sundays when we had a roast, she would pour the fat from the cooked joint into the chip pan. The chips acquired a smoky and crispy flavour that was simply heavenly. The only culinary aspect my mother struggled with was pastry. On occasion, I would visit a friend on Sundays, whose mother, Mrs Wright, baked apple pies that turned out thick and pale but delicious. I mentioned this to my mother, and the following week, she attempted to replicate Mrs. Wright's pie. However, her version turned out to be dark brown, thick, and unappetizing, despite her best efforts.

My father was a baker and each Sunday he would bring home anything unsold in the baker's shop. On Saturdays, we eagerly awaited a special treat - breaded ham served on a freshly baked loaf, slathered generously with creamy butter. This delightful combination became a cherished tradition.

I loved a Mandarin Cream Roll, a light and fluffy sponge roll filled with fresh cream and mandarins, offering a burst of delightful flavours with every bite. The festive season was particularly exciting as the mince pies took centre stage. The rich and spiced filling wrapped in buttery pastry made these pies a true holiday delight.

Drawing from his Lancashire heritage my father mastered the art of Eccles cakes, which were named after the town of Eccles. These flaky pastry delights filled with sweet currants were a treat. Another favourite was his Butter Pie, a delicious concoction originating from the Preston area. Its creamy potato and onion filling encased in buttery pastry was a comfort food loved by young and old alike.

Being an only child, I experienced my mother's battle with cancer at the age of five when she had to undergo a mastectomy due to breast cancer. When I turned 20 and had recently joined the police force, she never explicitly informed me but later revealed that if the cancer had recurred, she would have had to undergo a second mastectomy.

I remember going to the doctor on her behalf to collect some pills. The doctor inquired about her well-being, and when I responded truthfully, he burst into laughter because he understood my mother's nature. He remarked that she must have felt cheated in life, possibly due to her childhood experiences. Her illness began when my father was away at war, and she was only four and a half stone in weight due to her poor health. She visited the doctor, who callously dismissed her concerns, accusing her of self-pity and throwing her out of his surgery. At the time, my mother was caring for her friend Betty, who had contracted a severe flu. Coincidentally, the same doctor arrived, assuming it was my mother who was ill and not Betty. Upon seeing my mother's frail condition, he admitted her to the hospital the next day. She remained there for six months before undergoing the operation. They worked to restore her health as she was extremely emaciated. During that time, my grandfather relinquished his own house and moved in with us, otherwise, I would have likely ended up in an orphanage, as my father was serving in the war in India.

The surgery performed by Mr. Hooks involved the removal of her remaining breast and uterus in one procedure. The scars extended from her stomach to her breasts and along her back. In those days, such extensive scarring was the norm, unlike today where fine stitches are used. She was still quite young at the time. The surgery also involved addressing an issue with her bowels. I was 20 years old when she had her final mastectomy. She eventually opened up about it, mentioning that she had experienced the same pain and sensation as before. Afterwards, the doctor who operated on her became our family doctor, and we resolved the previous conflict. He was an Irish man with a great sense of humour, though often inebriated. I experienced several childhood illnesses, and he would visit in the morning to administer streptomycin injections. The injections would smell of whiskey, and he would occasionally stumble and fall onto the bed. He would drive to our house, which was common practice at the time, but he was a good old-fashioned doctor.

CHAPTER FIVE

THE UNCONVENTIONAL IMMUNITY - A LIFE OF RAW ONIONS

My mother had never fallen victim to a common cold or flu, a feat that puzzled both her family and medical professionals. However, it was during her stay in the hospital for cancer treatment that her immune resilience garnered attention. The hospital staff, amazed by her medical history, invited her to participate in a study to understand the underlying reasons for her seemingly invulnerable health.

Enthusiastically, she agreed to take part in the study, which involved a battery of tests and an in-depth dietary analysis. Her condition was indeed extraordinary, as she had never experienced any cold or flu-like symptoms, even during the most virulent seasonal outbreaks.

As the study progressed over her five-month hospital stay, the atmosphere with the nurses became light-hearted due to her unusual request. To maintain her daily ritual, she convinced the nurses to provide her with a raw onion every single day. This unique preference for raw onions amused the nursing staff, and they gladly obliged her endearing demand.

Later in her life her daily menu reflected her preference for simplicity, as she wasn't particularly fond of lavish meals. For her evening tea, she would typically indulge in slices of cheese, raw onion, and two slices of bread, a humble yet satisfying combination.

The medical team meticulously analysed the data collected during the study, and a prevailing pattern began to emerge. The doctors surmised that her consistent consumption of raw onions might be a crucial factor contributing to her remarkable immune system and overall robust health. I followed my mother's peculiar habit and I embraced the practice of consuming raw onions regularly. Despite occasional remarks from acquaintances about the onion scent, I firmly believed in the health benefits associated with this unique habit.

Chapter Six

COMPLEX FAMILY DYNAMICS AND PERSONAL STRUGGLES

S tarting with my first job as a clerk in a solicitor's office, I quickly realised that my wages were not entirely my own. My mother would retain most of my earnings, leaving me with a mere 5 shillings per week. To supplement my income, I worked at a prominent milk bar a few nights a week. The bar's owner, an ex-army captain, was a generous soul who would occasionally provide food for free. He had witnessed the deprivation during the war in Germany and firmly believed that no one should go hungry. I would often enjoy my dinner at the bar's cafe upstairs, indulging in the atmosphere of music before the place closed around 1 o'clock. The owner would even drop me off at my door, showcasing his kind-hearted nature.

Driven by a desire for personal expression and limited financial support, I attended night school to learn sewing, as I yearned for fashionable clothes. In the vibrant town of Blackburn, was a large and bustling market. Among the market's prominent features was the renowned firm, Horrocks, which became known for its exquisite fabrics available at discounted prices. I would frequently visit the market in search of beautiful materials for my creations.

With a flair for fashion, I would craft relatively simple yet elegant dresses. My designs featured side darts and a square neck at the back; the patterns were easy and I fashioned a new dress in just a single evening.

The market itself was a hub of activity, and it was easy to spot due to the campanile-style clock tower that stood tall at 72 feet. Crowned with a time ball, this tower served as a reliable timekeeper, dropping at precisely 1 p.m. daily, accompanied by the firing of a gun. This daily ritual left no room for excuses when it came to keeping track of time.

Interestingly, the presence of such an elaborate clock tower was deemed unusual for a town like Blackburn. However, the Markets Committee believed it was necessary due to the irregularities and discrepancies among public clocks in the area. The need for prompt punctuality in certain instances led to the approval of the clock tower's construction.

Reflecting on significant events, I recall an accident I had at 18 years old. I was standing at a traffic light when a car reversed, parking directly on my foot. Although the driver quickly moved the vehicle, my foot suffered severe injuries. I received compensation of £780, but my parents redirected the funds toward a new house when we moved. It struck me recently that I never saw a penny of that compensation, a testament to the different dynamics and expectations surrounding finances during that time.

Chapter Seven

Melodies and Memories: A Musical Journey in Lancashire

Our home on the outskirts of Woolacombe, Lancashire, was just 20 miles away from Blackpool, where big bands frequently performed. The Empress and Palace ballrooms in Blackpool served as a launching pad for local talents, who later gained nationwide fame. Among the notable maestros were Geraldo and his orchestra, with Ted Heath as their trombonist, and Joe Loss, whose influential musical careers were shaped by their Blackpool experiences.

At the age of 18, my parents finally allowed me to stay out late on Friday nights, thanks to the late-night buses that safely brought me home. My mother urged me to take the long route, but I often opted for a shortcut through the allotments to reach our house quickly, unbeknownst to her. Looking back, I realize the potential danger I put myself in.

During those days, I frequently encountered a kind lad named William. He was 20 and always offered me a ride home, dropping me off a block away from my house to avoid waking my father with the sound of motorbikes. Tragically, he lost his life in an accident while going to work the next morning, swerving to avoid a rabbit on the road.

Before hitting the dance halls, we would visit the fairground, I knew many people because they remembered me from working at the milk bar. We used to enjoy the rides for free. It was a delightful time filled with laughter and joy. One of the consistent highlights was the booth of Gypsy Rose Lee, which consistently drew a lengthy line of visitors. Establishing a connection with her during the fair unexpectedly resulted in an invitation to her exquisitely decorated trailer, featuring a sumptuously comfortable leather sofa. Another prominent figure from that era was the suave and sophisticated Dennis Lotus, a singer who embodied the style of Tony Bennett. In the year 1955, Dennis Lotus enjoyed immense popularity and captivated audiences with his smooth, velvety voice. His performances were unforgettable, leaving a lasting impression on all who had the pleasure of listening to him. Other famous artists and big bands performed in various venues including the Empress and Palace Ballrooms. Among the crowd's favourites was the renowned Joe Loss and his orchestra, and my friends and I were thrilled to be part of his enthusiastic fan base. We managed to secure seats in the dress circle during his performances, allowing us an exceptional view of the stage.

As the Teddy Boys infused their style into the music scene, two individuals stood out: Alan Walmsley and Peter Wallace. They reigned supreme in terms of dressing. The Teddy boys would confidently showcase their fashion sense, and these two young men, Alan and Peter, were exceptional in this regard. They were pleasant individuals, and there were no issues with them as they exhibited their presence and style. The dance halls where the big bands played were a hub of excitement and camaraderie. The seating arrangements were gender-specific, with girls occupying seats on one side and boys on the other. When the music began, couples would quickly pair up and dance together with joy and enthusiasm, creating a lively and spirited atmosphere.

Amidst the music and laughter, one particular gentleman, fondly known as Frank used to say "Come on, Irene," He was known for his charisma and persistence, often extending an invitation with a charming smile, encouraging me to dance with him. Although I occasionally obliged, my heart always yearned for the carefree and thrilling moments spent with the other dancing partners.

Looking back now, it's hard to believe that all these cherished memories took place, almost six decades ago. The vibrant energy, the enchanting music, and the camaraderie among friends and strangers alike continue to live on in my heart, serving as a reminder of the rich tapestry of experiences that define our lives. Those times were truly magical, and the melodies of Joe Loss and the sophisticated presence of Dennis Lotus are etched forever in the corridors of Lancashire's musical history.

Later on, after joining the police I had the pleasure of knowing a bunch of young folks who were fans of a little-known band called the Quarry Men. Little did we know, those four lads were destined for greatness and would later be known as the world-famous Beatles. I remember visiting Lytham town hall one evening and sneaking backstage to catch a glimpse of them before their performance. The air was buzzing with excitement, and you could sense there was something special about them. As soon as they took the stage and started playing, it was evident that they had that magic touch. Look at them now, who would have thought?

Chapter Eight

REACHING ADULTHOOD AND FAMILY DYNAMICS

F amily dynamics were complicated, and my mother rarely opened up or expressed affectionate sentiments. She had conflicts with my granddad and her brother, driven by jealousy and a desire for my grandmother's undivided attention. I distinctly recall my granddad's words, noting that my mother's behaviour didn't align with that of the Irish, who were generally more affectionate.

When I suffered from appendicitis and my appendix burst, I underwent surgery and stayed in the hospital.

My father had been battling cancer at the time, and the next day, while I was still recovering from the operation and had stitches all over, I had to drive to the Lake District because my father was scheduled for an operation three days later. The following morning, my mother yelled up at me while I was still asleep, without any thoughtfulness, She demanded bread! I reluctantly got up, and got myself dressed, to drive to the shop to buy a loaf Upon coming back, I inquired why she hadn't personally gone to our shop, especially since it was brimming with bread, and she replied with a hurtful remark, asking why I hadn't bought two loaves. She often said things to intentionally hurt others. I informed her that I was going to see my dad, and she insisted on accompanying me. Firmly, I told her that I would go on my own and proceed with my journey. When I visited my father and informed him about the incident with the bread and my appendicitis, he was in bed and unable to get up. I jokingly asked him how he managed to tolerate my mother for all those years. He replied that she was a good woman, albeit everything being black and white with her, while I was a perpetual shade of grey.

When it came to paying bills, I preferred to wait until I received a final demand before taking action. However, my mother found this approach to be appalling. If she received an electric bill on Wednesday, she would promptly pay it on Thursday. My father did whatever it took to maintain a peaceful atmosphere at home but was no match for her strong personality. I'm unsure how they met, but my mother often mentioned that she was pure when she went to the altar. While tempted to respond rudely to her claim, I refrained from doing so. In those times, purity held great significance, particularly in the 1920s and 1930s. Looking back, I realise how absurd it was.

CHAPTER NINE

MY GRANDFATHER RUNNING AWAY AND IN HIS LATER YEARS

My grandfather had fled Ireland after impregnating my grandmother when she was only 16 years old. The shame they brought upon the family necessitated their relocation to Scotland, where they stayed with my grandfather's younger brother. In my recollections of him during his later years, he presented himself as a charismatic Irishman with a penchant for indulging in drinks. He had white curly hair and piercing blue eyes that left a lasting impression. I remember my mother telling me how he immediately developed a strong bond with me as a baby, which came as a pleasant surprise. Every Saturday and Sunday, he would take me out in the pram and accompany me to the pub. When I questioned my mother about allowing him to take me along, she explained that she couldn't have prevented him from doing so. She mentioned that she never dared to object, but he frequently took me out on his outings. As I grew older, he even came to stay with me in Kirkby later in his life.

My mother invited my grandfather to stay with us in Kirkby, emphasizing that it was a pleasant area where one could enjoy a few drinks at the pub and safely walk home without any disturbances. I affectionately called my grandfather "Pop" and warned him to be cautious about mentioning that I was a police officer to the local pub regulars that he had become friendly with. They gathered in the local snug room at the back of the pub. He took pride in my career choice and a few nights before he left, I promised to take him out. However, being a hard drinker, my granddad could easily drink them under the table. He became friends with a lot of the local men and women at the pub enjoying many evenings in their company.

During my grandfather's funeral, my mother commented on the women present which nearly caused me to erupt in laughter. One of the women approached her and expressed that my grandfather was a true gentleman. Under her breath, my mother muttered a less favourable comment about the woman. She seemed to enjoy playing the bereaved daughter. After the funeral, another woman came up to us and suggested going to the pub to celebrate my grandfather's life and memory. This infuriated my mother. My father, lacking the courage to confront her, stood there silently. I once asked my father how he managed to tolerate her all those years without losing his temper.

Chapter Ten

FAMILY TRAGEDIES AND RESILIENCE

M y father was one of nine siblings, and some complexities arose within the extended family. My mother chose to distance herself from her father's side of the family, as she found them to be unpleasant individuals. However, I liked them, especially my Aunt Dora and her family, whom, I often visited Despite their rough edges, I felt a connection with them, and Aunt Dora and her family were cherished figures in my life.

The family encountered profound tragedy on a sombre Christmas Day when my father's parents passed away. Shockingly, my grandfather succumbed to a heart attack at lunchtime, followed by my grandmother's passing due to the same cause at teatime. The heartbreaking loss was further compounded when their daughter, who had never married and lived with them, tragically took her own life the following year in May. This series of devastating events took an immense toll on the family's emotional well-being.

After the losses, tensions arose among the remaining family members. A distressing incident occurred when one of the aunts approached my father, urging him to claim any possessions from the family home before others could take them. This led to a heated confrontation, and my father decided to sever ties with the rest of his relatives, choosing to distance himself from what he perceived as disgusting behaviour.

Reflecting on happier times, the family fondly recalls their paternal grandparents' home near the river Lune, where each child was assigned weekly household chores. One sibling was responsible for cleaning the school shoes, while another collected driftwood from the tidal river for the fire. The grandmother was known for her excellent culinary skills and a warm, matronly personality that endeared her to the family.

CHAPTER ELEVEN

REDISCOVERING IRISH ROOTS: A JOURNEY TO MY GREAT UNCLE RYAN'S HOME

M y great uncle, Ryan, lived in the picturesque west of Ireland in a place called Mayo, where he had constructed an English-style house. Fond memories of visiting him still linger in my mind. Behind the house, a vast field stretched out, alongside a stream that flowed through the rocks, providing a constant source of clear spring water for daily use.

During our travels across Ireland, we marvelled at the country's beauty, appreciating its allure as a fabulous place to explore. However, I couldn't help but reflect on the challenging times the Irish faced during the Great Famine. Many of my ancestors, like countless others, sought new opportunities in distant lands like New Zealand, Australia, and America, leaving behind their homeland and often losing touch with their roots.

 At my great uncle's place, tales of poteen, an illegal whiskey or moonshine, were shared, recounting how it was made using the purest spring water. Customs men occasionally patrolled the area, but they were carefully monitored from afar and could be seen approaching the family farm, giving them time to conceal the poteen. My great, great-grandmother ingeniously disguised the hidden barrel as a chair with a backrest, comfortably sitting on it with a rug draped over her knees when the customs officials conducted their searches. This clever ruse allowed them to sell the poteen discreetly, supplementing their income while keeping the village folk content.

As my grandmother grew older, she recounted stories from a troubled time when tensions ran high between the North and South of Ireland. During that period, the jails in Belfast were emptied of prisoners, causing unrest and instability. She shared a tale about one of her uncles, who was said to be mentally challenged. According to folklore, he was tied to a donkey's hooves and sent up into the mountains during the upheaval. Though such tales were not entirely accurate, they reflected the oral traditions and exaggerated narratives of those times.

In recent years, there has been a resurgence of interest in ancestral heritage, with many individuals reconnecting with their Irish roots by purchasing and restoring old family houses and farmhouses. This trend highlights the enduring love and longing for a connection to the land of their forefathers, honouring the legacy of the past and embracing the spirit of Ireland's rich cultural history.

CHAPTER TWELVE

UNVEILING THE DUCHESS – MY MOTHER IN HER LATER YEARS

Tragedy struck when my father passed away, and my mother came to live with us in our spacious old Victorian house with five bedrooms. To ensure her comfort, we arranged a bedroom upstairs for her, accompanied by a large sitting room adjacent to it. During this period, she remained content, finding fulfilment in volunteering twice a week for Oxfam. My mother was generally reserved and kept to herself, not letting many people into her inner circle.

As she grew older, my mother's health declined, and in the final three months of her life, she moved into an old people's home. It was during this time that her unique personality became obvious, known as the "Duchess," she displayed airs and graces, acting with refinement and elegance. Though she remained withdrawn, her distinct charm left a lasting impression on those who interacted with her during her final days.

As my mother assumed the role of the "Duchess" during her time at the old people's home, I couldn't help but feel a sense of sympathy for her. It seemed as though she was constantly projecting a false image, hiding her true self behind a facade of refinement and elegance. Deep down, I knew that she wouldn't openly participate in a conversation with just anyone. I believe that her upbringing, particularly under my strict grandfather's influence, might have played a significant role in shaping her personality and choices.

It was evident that there was tension between my grandmother and my grandfather, and he didn't hold a favourable opinion of her. The strain in their relationship might have affected her deeply, leading her to build a protective shell around herself, even during her final years. The emotional burden of knowing that my grandfather disliked her must have taken a toll on her self-esteem and sense of self-worth.

While I wished for my mother to feel free to express her true feelings and thoughts without the need to maintain the Duchess persona, I also understood that her behaviour was a result of complex and deep-rooted emotions. Despite the barriers she had built, I tried to support her and be there for her during her time at the old people's home.

As I reflect on her life and the challenges she faced, I realize that we all carry the imprints of our past experiences and relationships. Although my mother's journey was marked by a certain degree of emotional complexity, I appreciate some of the memories of the moments we shared, and I am grateful for the time we had together as a family. Even amidst the intricacies of human emotions.

CHAPTER THIRTEEN

THE PARANORMAL AND SPIRITUAL ENCOUNTERS

I magine my mother, a fashion-forward woman, donning a vibrant green suit with a velour trilby-style hat. We nicknamed her the "upside-down Tulip" for her unconventional style. Little did we know that this playful moniker would come back to haunt us in the most unexpected way.

Fast forward to a day when my daughter, Lucy attended a seance with some friends. Now, my mother had already passed away by this time. To her utter astonishment, the medium doing the seance said he had received a message, and he asked does an "upside-down tulip mean anything to you"? How indeed would the man know that we had called her such a name! He wanted Lucy to meet him afterwards, he said he had a message for her, but she did

not want to stay behind. She called me the following day fear palpable in her voice, she plead-
ed that we must stop calling my mother the "upside-down Tulip." Perplexed, she enlightened
me with the story and Lucy was spooked to her core. How could the medium have known
about our nickname unless there was some otherworldly communication happening? The
incident left us all dumbfounded, contemplating the mysteries of the afterlife.

But the supernatural encounters didn't stop there. When I was a child while riding on a
bus with my mother, a woman seated next to her began shuddering uncontrollably in an
eerie turn of events, she said you are very receptive to the spirits, she invited my mother to a
meeting at her home that evening. My poor mother was scared witless and promptly got off
the bus at the next stop, seeking refuge from the unexpected invitation.

The ties to the supernatural seemed to run in our family. My great-grandmother, hailing
from the beautiful landscapes of western Ireland in Mayo, was reputed to possess the gift
of foresight. She attended meetings and even entered trances, delving into the depths of the
unknown.

In the pursuit of spiritual exploration, I once attended a seance with my mother, guided
by a medium who distributed cards to everyone present. While my mother could see a
beautiful flower on her card, I found myself staring at mere dots, unable to perceive the
image. The medium inquired about our experiences afterward, and when I admitted my
inability to see the flower, he explained that some individuals are more receptive to such
visions than others.

Seeking healing for my back, I turned to a woman who claimed to possess healing hands.
Sceptical, but open-minded, I decided to give it a try. To my surprise, during the session, I
could feel the energy coming from the ladies' hands directly onto the area in pain, it was a
comforting experience and my back has remained better until this day.

Once not long after my husband died, I perceived a shadow of my husband on the settee,
though it was a fleeting glimpse that I initially dismissed as imagination. However, upon
reflection, I realized I must have witnessed it, as the memory remained vivid.

Intrigued by the unexplained, I found myself drawn to watching ghost-hunting programs
on television. These shows utilized machines that could detect electrical activity and hinted
at the idea that we, as human beings, emit energy in various forms. Some individuals seemed
more adept at receiving messages from the spiritual realm, a phenomenon that fascinated
me deeply.

I recently encountered a man from Serbia who shared a remarkable story of his spiritual
awakening. He claimed that God had spoken to him one day while he was alone on a

road in Serbia, urging him to change his ways. When asked about my beliefs in God, I admitted to believing in a supreme energy of some kind. This man eventually came to Spain and embarked on a life-changing journey, even starting his own company. He put my air conditioner in, and I couldn't help but marvel at the extraordinary path he had chosen.

Throughout my life, these experiences have opened my eyes to the mysteries of the spiritual realm and the power of human connection to the unseen forces. While scepticism often lingers, I have learned to approach such encounters with an open mind and a willingness to embrace the unknown. Each experience has left an indelible mark on my journey, reminding me that there is much more to this world than meets the eye. As I continue to explore the depths of spirituality and the unexplained, I remain in awe of the complexities and wonders that lie beyond our comprehension.

Through these humorous and extraordinary tales, I've come to believe that there is more to our existence than meets the eye. The afterlife, the world beyond our mortal realm, holds mysteries yet to be unravelled. My family's encounters with seances, the inexplicable knowledge possessed by mediums, and the legacy of my great-grandmother all hint at a reality beyond the tangible.

Chapter Fourteen

FACING INDEPENDENCE: FROM DOMESTIC LIFE TO LANCASHIRE'S FIRST CID POLICEWOMAN

In a household where my mother found contentment in cooking, cleaning, and caring for the dogs, I yearned for a different path—a life filled with purpose and adventure. Determined to make something of myself, I quietly applied for the position of a policewoman in Kirkby without disclosing my intentions to my parents.

Stepping into the unknown, I attended the first two interviews, still keeping my secret hidden. The interviews took place in Preston, and to my delight, I received a letter of acceptance. However, fate had an unexpected twist in store for me—my mother, ever curious, took it upon herself to open my mail. A commotion ensued as she confronted me, accusing me of seeking this opportunity solely to escape the confines of home.

Undeterred by the family turmoil, I joined the police force, ready to embark on a new chapter in my life. Little did I know that this decision would mark a significant milestone in the history of Lancashire's law enforcement. I became the first CID policewoman in the region, breaking barriers and paving the way for other women to follow.

The journey ahead was challenging, as being a female officer in a predominantly male environment presented its own set of obstacles. Yet, armed with determination and a desire to prove myself, I embraced the responsibilities that came with the CID role. Through my diligence and commitment, I earned the respect of my colleagues and became an integral part of the team.

As the first CID policewoman in Lancashire, I contributed to the transformation of the force, bringing a fresh perspective and a different approach to investigations. It was a privilege to serve my community and help ensure justice for the victims we encountered.

Reflecting on that pivotal moment when I quietly pursued my ambitions, I am grateful for the opportunity to have broken free from the traditional roles society had assigned to women. By choosing a path that challenged conventions, I not only found fulfilment in my own life but also played a small part in paving the way for future generations of policewomen in Lancashire and beyond.

CHAPTER FIFTEEN

A DARTING JOURNEY: TRIUMPHS AND TRIUMPHS

G rowing up as an only child, my father and I found solace and camaraderie in the game of darts during the chilly winter evenings. Our kitchen proudly displayed a dartboard in a cosy nook, where I would spend an hour after school honing my skills under my father's watchful eye. In those days, entertainment options were limited, with no television to distract us, so darts became our cherished pastime.

As I embarked on my career in law enforcement, I discovered an unexpected opportunity - the chance to join the police dart team. Curiosity piqued, I decided to give it a shot. A coach trip to Birmingham marked my first taste of competitive play. Among the participants, a skilled policewoman Sergeant from Brighton stood out as a formidable opponent.

Despite her expertise and age advantage, I managed to keep my nerves in check and emerged victorious, surprising everyone, including myself.

The elation of that win stayed with me as I travelled to London for the darts tournament finals. Nerves and excitement mingled, and I must admit, I indulged in a few gin and tonics before the decisive games. In the final, I faced the challenge of tallying up my scores accurately, but fortunately, a helpful fellow player assisted with the counting. With precision, I hit every target I needed, securing my victory. That night, luck was on my side, and my darting prowess shone brightly.

Acknowledging my skill on the board, I remained humble, knowing that there were many more talented players in the circuit. The woman from earlier encounters displayed consistent brilliance, though it seemed nerves got the better of her in our crucial face-off.

Later, the local newspaper celebrated my success with a photograph of me proudly holding the champion's cup. It was an unforgettable moment, one that would forever be etched in my memory.

Darts continued to be a constant part of my life, and I often found myself playing in the familiar setting of Kirkby. Each match presented its unique challenges and opportunities for growth, and I treasured every experience on this darting journey.

CHAPTER SIXTEEN

DELICATE ASSIGNMENT: A FEMALE OFFICER'S DIPLOMACY

In the close-knit community of Kirkby, a man on parole had overstayed his weekend leave, causing a predicament for the local police officers. Fearing a potential altercation, they sought an alternative approach to bring him back to prison. Being the only female officer in the team, they turned to me, believing he wouldn't resort to violence against a woman.

Tasked with the responsibility, I headed to the man's residence, only to find out from his wife that he was at the local pub. Kirkby was a place where everyone seemed to know everyone else, including me, and as I walked into the pub, the familiar whistling of the "Z Cars" theme tune greeted me.

Approaching him at the bar, I discreetly spoke to him, reminding him that he was supposed to return to prison. He seemed uncooperative, asserting that he wouldn't leave the pub with me. Knowing I couldn't handle the situation alone, I agreed to his request to bring the car around the back of the pub.

As we got into the car, he cheekily thanked me for the ride, as it saved him from having to change buses multiple times. He was trying to avoid the consequences of not returning to prison, which would have resulted in a warrant being issued for his arrest and someone having to bring him to the police station.

In retrospect, his plan was cunning, but with a diplomatic resolution, I managed to escort him back to Walton Prison safely. This incident highlighted the challenges and creative problem-solving that sometimes came with my role as a police officer, where delicate situations required finesse and quick thinking.

CHAPTER SEVENTEEN

HANDLING DRUNKEN ALTERCATIONS: A POLICE OFFICER'S EXPERIENCE

During my time as a police officer, encounters with women who required arrest were relatively rare, except for those under the influence of alcohol. One particular incident stands out vividly in my memory, where I found myself facing an aggressive and intoxicated young woman.

She had been causing a commotion, shouting and swearing, while confined to a cell after her arrest by a fellow officer. The noise and chaos prompted me to intervene and attempt to calm her down. However, in the heat of the moment, she lashed out and struck me with force.

In response, I made a regrettable decision and struck her back. The impact left a visible mark on my face. In hindsight, I knew it wasn't the appropriate course of action for a police officer, but the intensity of the situation clouded my judgment.

Interestingly, when it came time to document the incident and press charges, the young woman accused me of retaliation, claiming that I had hit her first. Though I denied the accusation, the circumstances made it challenging to pursue an assault charge against her.

When her mother arrived to collect her daughter from the station, I shared my side of the story with her. Surprisingly, her mother's reaction was unexpected as she expressed that her daughter deserved a sound punishment for her unruly behaviour.

It was evident that dealing with intoxicated women proved to be just as challenging, if not more so, than handling drunken men. Their behaviours and language could be especially volatile, making the situation demanding to manage for law enforcement officers.

This incident served as a valuable lesson in managing confrontations and maintaining professionalism, even under the most trying circumstances. As a police officer, I came to appreciate the importance of restraint and level-headedness when dealing with individuals who were under the influence and prone to aggression.

CHAPTER EIGHTEEN

A TRUE ACCOUNT OF A RAPE CASE

I n my career as a police officer, I encountered a distressing case of rape that left a lasting impact on me. The incident involved a family from Bootle, and the victim was a young 16-year-old girl who had attended a wedding.

After the wedding, a young man, whom she knew, offered to give her a ride home on his motorbike. However, he took advantage of the situation and stopped the motorbike at an isolated spot, where he sexually assaulted her against her will. Once the girl returned home, she mustered the courage to confide in her parents, who immediately reported the heinous crime to the police.

The father, consumed with anger and seeking retribution, set off to find the perpetrator himself, intending to deliver his own form of justice. Meanwhile, the victim bravely provided a detailed statement to the police, crucial for building a strong case against the assailant.

When the police located the young man, he displayed a defiant and uncooperative demeanour during questioning. Although the rape itself had not involved physical violence, it was evident that the victim had expressed her objections, and the young man had ignored her pleas. While some may argue that there was an element of mutual consent, the point at which she protested should have been respected.

The justice system prevailed, and the young man was sentenced to four years in prison for his actions. Inside the correctional facility, rapists are often subjected to harsh treatment by other inmates, reflecting the severity of the crime and the abhorrence it incites among prisoners.

This tragic incident served as a stark reminder of the immense responsibility entrusted to law enforcement officers. It reinforced the importance of conducting thorough investigations, respecting victims' statements, and ensuring that perpetrators face appropriate consequences for their actions. As a police officer, it was heartbreaking to witness the devastating impact such crimes have on the lives of victims and their families. Yet, it also motivated me to relentlessly pursue justice and offer support to those who had experienced unspeakable trauma.

CHAPTER NINETEEN

UNEXPECTED DUTIES: NAVIGATING THE BLACK MARIAH

O n one eventful day, I received an unusual task that I would never forget. I had to make a trip to court when I learned that the regular police driver for the notorious Black Mariah was unavailable. Due to my completion of the advanced driving course, I was the only eligible officer to drive this mysterious vehicle.

The Black Mariah, a large transit van with its windows blacked out, was typically used for transporting prisoners. Clad in a suit and high-heeled shoes, I mustered determination to climb into the van, a feat that proved more challenging than I anticipated.

In the back of the Black Mariah were six or seven prisoners, awaiting transfer to Walton prison. It was my responsibility to transport them safely to the facility, located in Liverpool City Centre.

Upon arrival at the prison, things took an unexpected turn. The sergeant instructed the prisoners to undress and proceed to the shower units. To my dismay, the men seemed uncomfortable with my presence, the men were shown little respect for the situation. The warden also appeared unconcerned, leaving the prisoners feeling embarrassed and vulnerable.

As I sat there, holding a newspaper, I couldn't help but feel uncomfortable, witnessing their loss of dignity. It struck me as wrong, even though I understood that this duty was typically performed by male officers. The prisoners likely did not anticipate a policewoman driving the Black Mariah, adding to their surprise.

While the prisoners showered, the warden delayed giving them their prison uniforms. The awkwardness persisted, and I found myself in the unique position of waiting for seven naked men to get dressed.

Once the prisoners were finally settled in their cells, it was time to leave the prison. Climbing back into the Black Mariah proved to be a challenge yet again, and an officer had to assist me in getting back on the seat. Unfortunately, during the process, my skirt rode up, unintentionally revealing my knickers.

To my mortification, I suddenly heard wolf whistles from the prisoners in their cells. It dawned on me that they could see me through the van's windows, making it an exceedingly embarrassing experience.

Thankfully, I completed the task without further incident and returned the Black Mariah safely. It was an unforgettable adventure, as a petite officer, driving the Black Mariah proved to be particularly difficult, thankfully, I never had to undertake that specific assignment again.

Chapter Twenty

A COMICAL MISHAP ON KIRBY TRADING ESTATE

One night, during my time as a police officer, I experienced a rather humorous and unusual incident that still brings a smile to my face whenever I recall it. I had just finished my shift and was off duty when I received an unexpected call asking me to return to the station urgently. They had encountered a distressed girl on Kirkby Trading Estate, an area known for its factories and frequented by courting couples.

Two fellow police officers, Bill and another one named Scott, were on patrol when they noticed a parked car. Curiosity got the better of them, and they decided to check on the occupants inside. To their surprise, they found a young girl in the back seat with no clothes on, accompanied by a young man.

As soon as the girl spotted the police officers, panic set in, and without thinking, she quickly exited the car and sprinted across a nearby field. It turned out that she recognized one of the officers as her next-door neighbour and feared that he would inform her parents about the situation.

Not knowing what else to do, the officer, Bill, sprang into action and chased after the girl. He managed to catch up with her and, despite her embarrassment, brought her back to the police station. The night was bitterly cold, and in a gesture of kindness, Bill lent her his coat to keep her warm.

The girl was understandably hysterical and frightened about what might happen next. But Bill assured her that he would not disclose anything to her parents and calmly spoke to her to calm her down. Slowly but surely, the girl began to regain her composure.

Meanwhile, back at the car, the young man handed over the girl's clothes to the police officers, revealing that she had left them behind. The situation was undeniably comical in its absurdity – an 18-year-old girl, scantily clad, running away with only her high-heeled shoes on and a handbag in hand.

As the events unfolded, it was hard not to find humour in the situation, but at the time, it was an utterly hysterical and surreal scene. Thankfully, the girl's panic subsided, and she was reunited with her clothes and belongings. While it was undoubtedly an amusing anecdote, it also served as a reminder of the unpredictable and light hearted moments that could arise during the course of our duties as police officers.

CHAPTER TWENTY-ONE

UNRAVELLING THE COMPLEXITY OF DOMESTIC VIOLENCE

I n my time as a police officer, one of the most challenging aspects of the job was dealing with domestic violence cases. One particular family frequently required our intervention, and I often found myself summoned to the home of a doctor and his wife.

Their household was marred by continuous domestic disputes, with the wife unleashing verbal abuse while the doctor remained silent, aggravating the already tense atmosphere. In those times, it was more difficult for couples to part ways compared to the present, where separation has become more commonplace and less stigmatized.

As I continued to respond to their distress calls, I gradually discerned that their issues extended beyond the surface conflicts. The root of their troubles lay in a sexual problem: the wife felt oversexed while the husband experienced the opposite, feeling undersexed. This stark contrast in their sexual desires led to constant clashes and escalating tensions.

Recognizing the complexity of the situation, we decided to seek professional help for the couple. Our department wrote to the local health authority, requesting counselling services for the troubled pair. Taking part in counselling sessions together would provide them with the opportunity to confront their issues in a safe and supportive environment.

Over time, the counselling sessions proved to be a turning point for the couple. The therapeutic interventions helped them address their sexual differences and understand each other's perspectives better. The doctor and his wife gradually began to communicate openly and work towards resolving their problems.

As progress was made, the doctor was eventually transferred out of Kirkby, which inadvertently provided a fresh start for the couple. They decided to move away to another town, leaving their tumultuous past behind and embracing the opportunity for a new beginning.

This case was a poignant reminder of the intricacies and underlying factors that can contribute to domestic violence. By approaching the situation with empathy, understanding, and the right resources, we were able to support this family on their journey towards healing and reconciliation. The experience reaffirmed my belief in the importance of providing individuals with the help they need to overcome challenges and foster healthier relationships.

CHAPTER TWENTY-TWO

POLICING IN SAFER TIMES:
REFLECTIONS ON KIRBY'S PAST

During my time as a police officer in Kirkby, the drug scene was notably different from the current landscape. Drug use was not as prevalent, and while the occasional cannabis cigarette or "spliff" could be found, no significant drug dealers were operating in the area. Liverpool, on the other hand, had a more pronounced drug presence with larger-scale dealers.

Fortunately, Kirkby remained relatively untouched by serious crimes, and murder cases were exceptionally rare. In contrast to today's distressing trends of knife-related incidents involving youngsters, violent crimes were significantly lower back then.

However, one unforgettable night marked a tragic event in the town's history. A fellow police officer lost his life during a fight outside a pub. I was off duty one evening and having just emerged from the shower, I found myself receiving an unexpected call, demanding all off-duty officers were called to the scene of the incident.

The officer had been struck during the altercation, and despite the immediate response to the incident, he did not survive. However, upon further investigation, a surprising discovery emerged during the post-mortem examination. It was found that the officer had an unusually thin skull, making him more vulnerable to fatal injuries. The medical experts concluded that even a single blow could have resulted in his untimely death.

Although no further action was taken in the case due to this revelation, the loss of a fellow officer left a profound impact on everyone in the force. It was an unfortunate incident of bad luck, highlighting the inherent risks that police officers face in the line of duty.

Reflecting on Kirkby's past, I am reminded of the town's comparatively safer environment and the sense of camaraderie among its residents. While policing has its challenges, my experiences in Kirbky taught me the importance of vigilance, adaptability, and supporting one another as a close-knit community.

CHAPTER TWENTY-THREE

THE MISSING SILVER: A TALE OF INDUSTRIAL OVERSIGHT

During my time as a police officer, one case that stands out prominently in my memory is the incident involving Otis Elevators, a prominent American firm with a factory in the area. The company manufactured valuable silver parts, which they kept unlocked, and this carelessness led to a series of thefts by their employees.

With approximately £3 million worth of silver left unsecured, it was an invitation for employees to pilfer the valuable material. Many workers took advantage of this lax security, leading to a significant amount of silver going missing from the factory.

My boss from the District Headquarters (DHQ) decided to take matters into his own hands. He confronted the American company representatives, expressing his dismay and criticism, stating, "You're running a charity here?" His remarks highlighted the absurdity of leaving valuable items unsecured, especially when the factory employees were not well-paid.

Following this incident, Otis Elevators realized their mistake and took immediate action. The remaining silver was placed under lock and key to prevent further thefts. The company's careless approach to security had been costly, but the changes they implemented demonstrated that they had learned from their mistake.

However, my boss's bold statement did not go without consequences. The American representatives took offence and reported him for his comment. Despite his intentions to raise awareness about security issues, he faced trouble for his forthrightness.

This incident shed light on the significance of addressing security loopholes within businesses and the role of law enforcement in holding companies accountable. It also highlighted the delicate balance between expressing concerns about security practices and the potential repercussions of doing so. Although the incident caused a stir and led to my boss facing some repercussions, it also served as a reminder of the importance of maintaining security measures to protect valuable assets. The case of Otis Elevators and the missing silver left a lasting impact on the factory's operations, influencing a change in their approach to security and the welfare of their employees.

CHAPTER TWENTY-FOUR

A TRAGIC ACCIDENT: WITNESSING THE UNFORESEEN

During my time as a police officer, I experienced a devastating event that left a lasting impact on me. One day, while I was questioning a woman for shoplifting on the first floor of the police station, I glanced out of the window and witnessed a heart-wrenching accident unfold before my eyes.

The police station's window overlooked a wide main road with a grass verge separating it. As I stood there, my attention was drawn to two women walking along the road, each accompanied by a small child. The children appeared excited and engaged in conversation with each other. Sadly, they were not holding the hands of the women, and this would lead to an unthinkable tragedy.

In a split second, the children, unaware of the imminent danger, suddenly darted into the road. A man driving along the road was unable to stop in time, and the unthinkable happened. He struck the children with his vehicle, resulting in a devastating accident.

As a witness to this horrific event, I felt an overwhelming sense of helplessness and sorrow. My thoughts often wandered back to those women, who were simply walking along, absorbed in conversation, with no inkling of the tragedy that would unfold.

The accident became a major news story, and the press covered it extensively. The community was shocked and deeply saddened by the loss of these innocent lives. It was an incident that left an indelible mark on the hearts of all who heard about it.

Reflecting on this tragic accident, I was reminded of the fragility of life and how a moment of distraction can lead to life-changing consequences. It underscored the importance of vigilance and mindfulness, especially when caring for young children.

Witnessing such a devastating accident reinforced my commitment as a police officer to promote safety and raise awareness about road safety measures. It also emphasized the significance of empathy and support for those affected by tragedies, as they navigate through unimaginable grief and loss.

CHAPTER TWENTY-FIVE

NAVIGATING THE CRIMINALITY OF SUICIDE ATTEMPTS

D uring my time as a police officer, the laws surrounding suicide attempts were vastly different from the present day. Attempting suicide was considered illegal at the time, which had significant implications for both the individuals involved and the police officers tasked with handling such cases.

If someone attempted suicide and survived, I would often find myself interviewing these individuals at the hospital. It was a delicate and challenging task, as we had to gather their statements and decide on the appropriate course of action. In most cases, we would recommend no further legal action, as the focus was on providing support and ensuring the individual's well-being.

Remarkably, during that era, it seemed that a majority of such cases involved women. These women were often burdened with numerous responsibilities, including caring for children, while struggling with financial hardships and relying on unemployment benefits. For some, managing money effectively was a significant challenge, leading to additional stress and desperation.

In my personal life, I witnessed how my parents coped with financial difficulties when my father was unable to work due to illness. My mother, skilled in budgeting and cooking, managed to make the most of the benefits they received, even saving up for a family holiday. Her resourcefulness and money management skills served as valuable lessons.

It was distressing to see that attempting suicide was a criminal offence, creating further distress for individuals already dealing with mental health issues. Many faced desperate situations, and discussing mental health openly was not as prevalent as it is today. Seeking help was not always straightforward, as mental health facilities struggled to cope with the demand. Furthermore, not all staff members working in the mental health division had received sufficient training to handle the various forms of mental health issues effectively.

Those working in mental health often found themselves thrown into the deep end, facing challenges beyond their training. As a result, individuals in need of support did not always receive the care and attention they required.

Reflecting on this chapter of history, it is evident how much progress has been made in terms of mental health awareness and support. Today, we are more open about mental health, and efforts are being made to improve facilities and training for mental health professionals. Nonetheless, there is still work to be done to ensure that everyone has access to adequate and compassionate mental health care. As we move forward, it is essential to continue striving for a society that understands and supports those facing mental health challenges, offering them the help and understanding they deserve.

Chapter Twenty-Six

EMBRACING IDENTITY AND LOVE

In my time as a police officer, I had the pleasure of working alongside a colleague named Joanne, who happened to be a lesbian. When she joined the police force at the age of 30, she quickly became a good friend to me. Curiosity got the better of me one day, and I asked her why she had never married. She cryptically replied, "I'll tell you someday."

Joanne's career took an exciting turn as she joined the traffic duty, where she was assigned to drive those striking white sports cars. During her training school days, she formed a close friendship with a female police trainee from another facility. At the time, I didn't fully understand the dynamics of their relationship and was quite naive about the concept of lesbianism.

Eventually, Joanne decided to transfer to the Manchester Division, where her life took an unexpected turn. She engaged in an affair with a married woman, her husband held a prominent position and had considerable wealth in the football field. Rumours of their relationship spread, and it caused a stir within the police force.

The married woman's husband threatened to expose Joanne's involvement with the married woman leading the police to face potential consequences. However, as there were no criminal offences some rules and regulations needed committed, and nothing was formally done about the situation.

As with any workplace, some rules and regulations need to be adhered to. For instance, whenever an officer left their section for more than 12 hours, they were required to notify their whereabouts. Joanne inadvertently overlooked this rule on one occasion, and it led to disciplinary action against her. Although she faced repercussions, she continued her relationship with the married woman, who eventually left her husband and returned to her hometown of Barry, where she started a driving school.

As time passed, my understanding of love, identity, and relationships evolved, and I learned to accept and support Joanne for who she was. Looking back on those days, I realize how much society and perceptions have transformed since then, embracing diversity and recognizing the importance of love and acceptance in all its forms.

Joanne's journey serves as a reminder that love knows no boundaries and that every individual deserves respect and understanding, irrespective of their sexual orientation. As the world continues to progress.

CHAPTER TWENTY-SEVEN

A DISTRESSING CASE AND THE LACK OF MENTAL HEALTH SUPPORT

In my career as a police officer, I encountered a deeply troubling case involving a young woman struggling with mental health issues. Whenever she neared a breakdown, she would write threatening letters to Harold Wilson, the MP at the time. Disturbingly, she expressed her intent to harm someone in these letters.

As soon as the letters reached the Kirkby station, it was our responsibility to respond to the situation. My fellow officer, John, who stood nearly 6 feet tall, bravely took on the task of visiting the woman's house. Another officer accompanied him for support.

When they arrived at her residence, the woman, amid a distressed episode, opened the door and invited them in. Tragically, in her agitation, she hurled faeces at them. Fortunately, the other officer managed to evade the assault, but John was not as fortunate and ended up covered in the unpleasant substance.

Following such incidents, the woman would often be placed under a section for approximately three weeks to a month. After receiving appropriate care and support, she would temporarily stabilize. However, her mental health challenges were persistent, and after 6 to 7 months, the cycle would repeat itself.

The situation was disheartening because mental health awareness and support were not as advanced as they are today. In those times, mental health struggles were not always fully recognized or understood, leaving individuals like this woman without the necessary support they needed.

The lack of recognition and understanding surrounding mental health led to a reluctance among people to speak openly about their struggles, for fear of being ridiculed or stigmatized. It was a sad reality of the times, but it also underscores the progress that has been made in the last decade in terms of mental health awareness and support.

As a police officer, this case was a stark reminder of the pressing need to improve mental health services and reduce the stigma surrounding mental health issues. Encountering such cases motivated me to advocate for better mental health resources and to approach each situation with empathy and understanding, recognizing the complexities of mental health challenges.

Chapter Twenty-Eight

Mastering the Night: A Gruelling Advanced Driving Course in Wales

In my time with the police force, advanced driving courses were a regular part of our training, and one particular course stands out in my memory—the advanced driving course in Wales. Spanning six weeks, this course focused on honing our driving skills, with a significant portion dedicated to night driving in challenging conditions.

The course instructor, Sergeant Baxter, had a reputation for being tough and demanding. Under his guidance, we embarked on night drives along winding mountain roads, where the darkness added an extra layer of difficulty. The vehicle assigned to me was a Ford Zephyr, a substantial car for its time. However, being of shorter stature, I faced the added challenge of adjusting the seat height and position to ensure optimal visibility.

Sergeant Baxter pushed us to our limits throughout the course. He constantly encouraged us to test our boundaries, urging us to push the accelerator further, straighten the car, and maintain higher speeds. Navigating those treacherous roads in the dark was nerve-wracking, and I often resorted to sitting on a pile of coats to elevate myself and improve my sight lines.

Despite the intensity of the training and the challenging conditions, I managed to complete the course without any accidents. It was a testament to the importance of regular testing and skill development for police officers. The advanced driving course not only honed our driving abilities but also sharpened our reflexes and decision-making skills in high-pressure situations.

Looking back on those six weeks, a sense of dread would often wash over me before each night drive. The demanding nature of the course and the dark, winding roads created a daunting environment. However, it was through these challenging experiences that I gained invaluable skills and confidence in handling difficult driving conditions.

The lessons learned during that advanced driving course stayed with me throughout my career in law enforcement. They emphasized the significance of ongoing training and the pursuit of excellence in serving and protecting the community. The ability to navigate challenging roads and make split-second decisions became essential tools in fulfilling my duty as a police officer. Courses such as this, emphasize the significance of ongoing training and the pursuit of excellence in serving and protecting the community.

CHAPTER TWENTY-NINE

UNVEILING THE DODGY GARAGE: A TALE OF CAR COVER-UPS AND CONSEQUENCES

A s a former police officer, I experienced firsthand the repercussions of having an accident in a police car. The standard punishment was a six-month grounding, effectively rendering the officer unable to drive. In the Criminal Investigation Department (CID), however, a different approach was taken. When officers encountered minor bumps or scratches in their vehicles, they would promptly cover up the incidents to avoid severe penalties.

Not far from Walton police station in Liverpool, there existed a notorious dodgy garage. This establishment became the go-to place for Liverpool city police officers who found themselves in need of repairs after a bump or a minor scratch. The mechanics at the dodgy garage had perfected the art of rejuvenating damaged cars, meticulously restoring them to their former glory. By doing so, they provided a lifeline to officers who would otherwise face grounding if the damages were discovered.

Among the officers at our station was Dave, who found himself in such a predicament. His car had suffered a front-end collision, and knowing the consequences of reporting it, he decided to avail himself of the dodgy garage's services. After the repairs were completed, the car returned to our station in Kirkby. Unbeknownst to me and the rest of the team, Dave had managed to keep the accident under wraps, as was customary among the officers.

However, fortune was not on Dave's side when he chose to park his car directly outside the police station upon his return. It was precisely at that moment that the traffic sergeant from our station made his appearance. I had just pulled in and observed the traffic sergeant engaging in a conversation with the inspector while casually leaning against Dave's Ford Anglia. As he rested his hands on the car's bonnet, I noticed a peculiar detail—brown paint staining his hands!

The traffic sergeant, entirely unaware of the incriminating evidence on his hands, unintentionally revealed Dave's attempt to conceal the accident. Sensing that something was amiss, the traffic sergeant reported the situation. Dave faced repercussions for his actions, including a month's deduction from his wages. It served as a stark reminder of the risks associated with trying to cover up accidents and the importance of integrity within the police force.

The incident with the dodgy garage and Dave's subsequent punishment highlighted the moral dilemmas and potential consequences that police officers faced in protecting their driving records. It underscored the significance of transparency and accountability within law enforcement, reminding us of the essential role that honesty plays in upholding the principles of the police force. Ultimately, Dave's ordeal served as a valuable lesson in the importance of integrity and ethical conduct in the face of difficult choices.

CHAPTER THIRTY

BARBARA'S EVENTFUL FIRST DAY AS A POLICE RECRUIT AT KIRBY

B arbara began her journey as a police recruit in Kirkby, and I had to accompany her. Her first day was filled with unexpected incidents. As we embarked on our patrol, she suggested making a quick stop for some shopping. While parked among a row of cars, I assumed the passenger seat, with Barbara taking the wheel. However, as we prepared to set off, the car was still in gear, resulting in a collision with the vehicle in front. The impact caused a milk bottle to explode, leaving me drenched.

Amidst the chaos, Barbara and I grew anxious, fearing repercussions and grounding for six months. They inspected the damage and noticed only a minor scratch on the bumper, but the car in front had a dent. A man approached us, and it became evident that the damaged car belonged to him. He expressed frustration, sharing that he had recently purchased the vehicle and hadn't even brought it home yet. He had already sent it for repairs twice before due to previous accidents. Overwhelmed, he sat down, lamenting how his wife would find it hard to believe that it had happened again. I reassured him that they would take the car to the garage for repairs, as the police car they were in was not damaged. Although Barbara's actions could have automatically grounded her, we managed to arrange for the necessary repairs.

Returning to work, I was still soaked in milk, my hair was flattened. When asked about my appearance, I explained the milk spillage incident during the collision. The damaged car owner's contact information was obtained to avoid involving the police station, as we had used our home address for communication. We accompanied him to the garage, and upon returning the car, his wife warmly welcomed them, with her primary concern being the condition of the vehicle.

Later, Barbara secured a council flat in Kirkby, as it was challenging to find Liverpool council properties. Police lodges were available at the police station, but they were primarily reserved for male officers. She became familiar with her new surroundings.

During a visit to the doctor, Barbara met a young doctor whom she eventually married. They had four sons, each born within ten months of one another. Her husband's family owned an oil company, and his father was a wealthy man. Over the years, Barbara maintained contact with me.

In their retirement, Barbara and her husband settled in Monte Carlo, attracted by his fondness for gambling. She became suspicious that he may have had another family in America due to his frequent visits. Barbara diligently observed her husband's behaviour, suspecting he had secrets, and eventually managed to unlock a suitcase that she believed contained evidence. Despite her continued doubts, she didn't find anything thank goodness.

She still retained a glamorous image. One memorable night, she attended a nightclub in Liverpool where she found herself seated with footballers from an opposing team. They generously passed drinks to her and her companions. Coincidentally, that same evening, a crew member from a popular detective TV show, The Bill, which was being filmed in Liverpool, was spotted and a sergeant who was with us pointed out an actor who portrayed a sergeant on the show, he said where do I know him from! The sergeant had recognized the actor but only as a police officer, not realizing he was an actor.

CHAPTER THIRTY-ONE

A FALSE COMPLAINT

One evening during my shift at the station, a woman entered, reporting that she had been a victim of rape. Given my limited encounters with genuine rape victims, her claim raised suspicions. Over the following month, it became evident that she frequently engaged in heavy drinking and made light-hearted jokes. It seemed possible that she used these tactics to avoid criticism from her husband for being late, relying on the perception that women are cunning and deceptive. However, I want to emphasize that such generalizations are unfounded and not applicable to all women.

In an attempt to gather more information, I involved a doctor, whose name escapes me but is recognized for his distinctive waxed moustache. As they entered the examination room, the doctor's approach lacked sensitivity. He requested the woman to remove her undergarments, making a remark about her alleged familiarity with doing so. During the examination, he lightly slapped her leg and confidently declared that she had never experienced rape.

Leaving the room due to the doctor's departure, I encountered a newly assigned police sergeant who wished to share an observation. He informed me that he had seen the woman at the back of the shops, eating chips. Confused, I questioned the relevance of this detail. The sergeant clarified that she was accompanied by a man, with her arms wrapped around his neck. It became evident that they were engaging in a consensual sexual encounter. The sergeant intervened, instructing them to stop and move along. When questioned about the man's response, he simply stated that he would not take much longer.

By this time, it was approximately 2:30 a.m. Detective Sergeant Smith, who was on duty, instructed me to accompany the woman back to her home and advised caution in informing her husband about the situation, considering the late hour. Upon arriving at their residence, I woke the husband, who was asleep in bed. It was notable that he appeared dishevelled, wearing worn-out underpants and a dirty vest that hadn't been washed in weeks, the house was very scruffy. I explained the urgency of the situation, informing him that his wife was in the car. Perplexed, he inquired about her actions, to which I clarified that she had made a rape allegation. He expressed frustration at her frequent claims and questioned the mention of fish and chips. I explained that she had been eating them while the incident was said to have occurred. He responded dismissively, showing little concern or jealousy, perceiving it as a trivial matter.

CHAPTER THIRTY-TWO

MEMORIES OF POLICE TRAINING AND HILARIOUS MISHAPS

During my time in the police force, we underwent a rigorous three-month training at the training school to ensure our fitness and preparedness. Part of the training included cross-country runs, but some of my colleagues discovered a sneaky shortcut through the woods. They would stop midway, have a cigarette, and wait for the rest of us to catch up, making it seem as if they completed the entire run.

One particular memory stands out from my last training course. I formed a close bond with two fellow trainees, Avril Tittering a talented singer and a social drinker, and Joanne

Brown, a tall and warm-hearted individual. One night, we ventured into a local bar in town, where Helen captivated the attention of the barman with her charming personality and striking appearance. Playfully, she helped herself to drinks from the optics behind the bar each time the barman left his station, passing one down to us all in a line.

Returning late to the training ground, we found ourselves locked out, leading us to climb over a wall to gain entry. Despite the challenges of my high heels and short skirt, I managed to make it over the wall. However, Joanne was caught by security guards and faced charges the following day. Two police officers escorted Joanne into the Detective inspector's office. When we met afterwards, she mentioned slipping on a mat.

Years later, as I worked at Rochfield Station, I met a Detective Inspector who recognized me from the training days. To my surprise, he revealed that he was the inspector who had to discipline Joanne. He recounted the incident; he said two policemen marched her up there it was a very formal affair. On entering the room the policeman marched her up to his desk and he said I had a rug in front of the desk as she stood up to attention, she slipped and finished up with the legs around his waist. "I said, what did you do"? He said I was dying to laugh, but I threw her out of the office. Although he managed to maintain a formal demeanour, he confessed that he couldn't help but burst into laughter once she left his office.

It wasn't all physical work during the training; we also dedicated significant time to studying law. Those three months proved to be hard-going as we absorbed the intricacies of legal principles and their application in real-life scenarios.

Subsequently, I had the opportunity to attend a four-month-long CID course at the training school, delving deeper into the complexities of detective work. The CID training involved setting up various situations, simulating arrests, and teaching us how to handle specific scenarios with precision and tact. While the training was still rigorous, it allowed for a slightly more relaxed atmosphere compared to the initial police training, which was incredibly regimented.

Interestingly, I found that my gender often worked to my advantage when making arrests. As a woman, my approach seemed to have a calming effect, diffusing tense situations without the need for an overpowering authoritative demeanour. The people of Liverpool, known for their warm-heartedness, responded well to the respectful and understanding approach, making the process of arresting individuals far smoother than one might expect.

Throughout my career, I had the privilege of working alongside good-hearted individuals in the Liverpool police force. The camaraderie among the officers was remarkable, and the city's residents were generally cooperative and understanding during arrests. This sense of community and cooperation among the people of Liverpool made it a fulfilling and rewarding experience to serve as a police officer in the city.

CHAPTER THIRTY-THREE

PARADISE STREET: LIVERPOOL'S SEAFARING LEGACY

As ships returned to Liverpool, its port became the gateway to Europe, attracting seafarers in search of entertainment. The street's association with brothels and strip clubs earned it the nickname "Paradise," street, drawing sailors looking for pleasures after long voyages. However, amidst this vibrant seafaring culture of Liverpool, Paradise Street offered sailors a taste of pleasure and entertainment, and the maritime culture also fostered an environment of diversity and cultural exchange.

During the 1950s, Liverpool's maritime trade remained a vital part of the city's identity. As ships docked at the bustling port, weary sailors from around the globe found themselves drawn to the enchanting streets of Liverpool, seeking amusement and camaraderie.

Paradise Street drew sailors with its lively establishments, including brothels and entertainment venues. For the seafarers arriving in Liverpool after their transatlantic journeys, Paradise Street became a haven of relaxation and pleasure.

Liverpool's maritime connections extended beyond adventure and entertainment. As ships voyaged to far-off lands in the early 20th century, they brought back exotic treasures, including the prized pineapple. At these times tropical fruits remained a rarity in Europe, often reserved for the wealthy elite who could afford such luxuries.

Even as time moved forward, the essence of Liverpool's maritime splendour continued to resonate with pineapples adorning select buildings that served as enduring symbols of Liverpool's seafaring past, a testament to the city's once-thriving trade and its global connections.

CHAPTER THIRTY-FOUR

HILARITY IN THE HARBOR: THE ADVENTURES OF SANDRA WHITE

B ack in the day, whenever those American ships docked, you could bet that the docks would come alive with a colourful cast of characters, including ladies of the night from all over the country. I had to go down to the docks to chat with these ladies and make sure they were doing alright. Let me tell you, those encounters led to some uproariously funny stories.

One of the ladies who stood out from the crowd was Sandra White. She had a rich old fella wrapped around her finger, and he would shell out a whole ten pounds for each session.

But here's the kicker - this old guy had a bit of a problem getting things up and running. So, Sandra being the resourceful gal she was, came up with a creative solution. She'd get his you-know-what into the crack of her thighs and give it a little squeeze, all while whispering sweet nothings like, "Oh, oh Mr. Jones, you're so forceful!" Classic Sandra!

Believe it or not, Sandra White had quite the rags-to-riches story. She ended up marrying an American gentleman, the son of a famous jeweller from sunny California. They had a string of shops, and their life seemed like something out of a fairy tale. Whenever I called in to check on Sandra's mother, she'd show me pictures of their jaw-dropping mansion in California. It was nothing short of elegant, with grandeur fit for royalty. And to think, it all started from a Liverpool girl making her way in the world.

Who would've thought that a plucky lass from Liverpool, once known for her escapades by the docks, would wind up as a millionaire's wife in California? It just goes to show that life's surprises can be funnier than fiction. Sandra White's journey from the docks to dazzling riches is a tale that still tickles me to this day. And as for those days down by the harbour, well, they provided me with stories that I'll be sharing for years to come.

Oh, those were wild times down at Liverpool Dock when the American ships would arrive! The influx of ladies of the night from all corners of the country would make sure of that. But you see, Liverpool Dock was no ordinary port. They knew all too well the temptations that awaited those sailors with their hard-earned money fresh from the ship's voyage. So, they had a clever trick up their sleeve - they wouldn't let the men take all of their money off the ship, just to protect them from losing it all to the cunning charms of those enterprising ladies.

And speaking of antics at the dock, there was one unforgettable case in Bootle that made it to the headlines. A massive ship pulled into Liverpool, delivering hundreds of wheelbarrows. Now, this ship stood in the dock for quite some time, giving the dock workers ample opportunity to hatch a plan. You see, those cheeky dockers would sneak onto the ship, one by one, and discreetly smuggle out one wheelbarrow at a time. The security officers aboard the ship had no clue what was happening, and the audacious dock workers kept nicking wheelbarrows right under their noses.

When the ship was finally ready to be unloaded, the truth was revealed - hundreds of wheelbarrows had mysteriously vanished! It was like a magic trick that had everyone scratching their heads in disbelief. But it wasn't magic at all; it was the ingenious and mischievous dockers at work, making off with those wheelbarrows like there was no tomorrow.

You see, life at the docks wasn't just about hard work and seriousness. It was a place where camaraderie and mischief often went hand in hand. Those dockers had a knack for finding a mischievous adventure in the most unexpected places. They turned mundane tasks into unforgettable escapades, leaving everyone, from fellow workers to the headlines, laughing and shaking their heads in disbelief.

Ah, those were the days when Liverpool Dock was never just an ordinary port; it was a vibrant stage for a colourful cast of characters, where even wheelbarrows could disappear without a trace, all thanks to the dock workers who knew how to leave their mark on history.

Chapter Thirty-Five

A WATCHFUL EYE AT LIVERPOOL DOCKS

When on watch at Liverpool docks, I had a crucial responsibility to look out for any suspicious characters. One day, my attention was drawn to two young Irish girls, who were unaccompanied by an adult. I knew all too well that the docks were a place where people would approach vulnerable young ladies and attempt to lead them into prostitution.

As I observed from a distance, I noticed a woman approaching the girls, her actions setting off alarm bells in my mind. Determined to ensure the girls' safety, I decided to approach the woman and question her about her connection to the girls. However, she was evasive and quickly hopped into a waiting car, a male driver at the wheel, leaving me with a sense of unease.

When I spoke to the girls, they said that they had only just met the woman. She had offered to look after them after one of them fell ill during their journey, they had just disembarked off a ship. It became evident that the woman had deceived them, falsely claiming that their eventual destinations were close to hers and suggesting they share a car.

Deeply concerned about the potential dangers the girls might face, I sought to understand why they were travelling so far from their homes and families in Ireland. To my relief, they informed me that they had secured jobs as nurse probationers at a hospital. However, it was apparent that they were unaware of the potential risks posed by seemingly well-meaning strangers.

Realizing the gravity of the situation, I couldn't help but worry about the many dangers these girls could encounter if left unprotected. Unaccompanied women and girls, especially those arriving from Ireland, were particularly vulnerable in large urban centres like Liverpool docks.

To address my concerns and ensure the girls' safety, I decided to reach out to the matron at the hospital where they were headed. The matron shared my apprehensions and was immensely grateful for my intervention. She requested that the police provide escort services for any other Irish girls who might be on their way to the hospital to protect them from potential harm.

As I reflect on that day, I am reminded of the importance of being vigilant and proactive in safeguarding the vulnerable. The docks can be a treacherous place, and I was relieved to have potentially saved these girls from the clutches of unscrupulous individuals. This experience only strengthened my resolve to continue protecting those in need and to remain watchful over the bustling port city of Liverpool

CHAPTER THIRTY-SIX

RESCUING RUNAWAY GIRLS ON THE EAST LANCASHIRE ROAD

A significant incident that occurred on the East Lancashire Road, involved the rescue of three runaway girls who had escaped from an approved school run by nuns. They aimed to make their way to Liverpool. During this encounter, I witnessed behaviour that astounded me. We arrived at the station with the girls, and one of them approached me with fear in her eyes. She revealed her apprehension about being locked in a dark cellar for a gruelling 12-hour period as punishment. It was remarkable to learn that this particular girl was only 15 years old, a mere five years younger than me. Despite their youth, these girls had already experienced a harsh reality and displayed a worldly attitude. It became evident that their troubled backgrounds had shaped their lives in significant ways. The nun arrived to take back the three runaway girls. Arrival of a Nun seeking assistance for the three runaway girls a black vehicle known as a Black Mariah made its presence known. Its doors swung open, and I witnessed a scene that caused alarm bells to go off in my head. The diminutive nun, considerably smaller than me, resorted to a forceful approach. She grabbed the 15-year-old girl by the collar and skirt, forcefully propelling her into the awaiting van. Without hesitation, she repeated the action with the other two girls. Concerned for their well-being, I inquired about any potential harm caused by the nun's actions. To my surprise, the nun brushed off my concerns, assuring them that the girls would be fine. With a resounding slam, the van's door closed, leaving unanswered questions about the true nature of the approved school and the methods employed there.

CHAPTER THIRTY-SEVEN

A SHOCKING INCIDENT AND AN INFAMOUS DETECTIVE

Shocking encounters that challenge one's perception of individuals in positions of authority. Here I recount the worst experience of my career, an incident that unfolded with a policeman in my car, and the subsequent downfall of an infamous detective named Peter.

Ken, a former colleague in the CID, played a significant role in my professional life. As my direct supervisor, he emphasized the importance of caution and provided guidance regarding Peter's behaviour during social outings. Ken advised me to exercise vigilance when spending time with Peter and the group, especially after consuming alcoholic beverages. He expressed concerns about Peter's tendency to become unpleasant towards women.

Intrigued, I sought clarification, prompting Ken to reveal that Peter engaged in peculiar actions. To ensure my safety, Ken suggested having someone closely monitor Peter's interactions when visiting venues such as clubs.

As a member of the CID, it was imperative to refrain from consuming alcohol while driving a police car. However, when there was a CID function, it often included a comedian, making for a memorable night out. Unfortunately, one particular evening turned into a nightmare. I had the responsibility of driving three policemen back after dropping off the first two. Little did I know that the remaining officer had something entirely different in mind.

As we travelled under the brightness of the moon, the officer abruptly requested that I stop the car. Assuming he needed a quick wee break, I was taken aback when he remained seated and began engaging in lewd behaviour, he was playing with himself. Shocked and appalled, I couldn't believe my eyes. In a disturbing turn of events, he even asked me for a handkerchief, which I reluctantly provided from my bag, he wiped himself down, zipped himself up and said That's better. I couldn't fathom the audacity of what had just transpired.

Upon returning to the police station to clock off, my distress was evident to the sergeant, who inquired about my well-being. Reluctantly, I divulged the shocking incident, expecting some understanding or support. Instead, he laughed and questioned why I didn't take action. In truth, I was paralyzed with shock, unable to comprehend the gravity of the situation. Had his advances escalated, I may have found the strength to confront him.

News of this unsettling episode reached the Chief Superintendent and the Detective Inspector, prompting them to urge me to report the incident to the superior authorities at HQ. However, my reservations were justified as Mr Martin, the Deputy Chief, had previously made inappropriate remarks, leaving me feeling uncomfortable and embarrassed. This history of suggestive behaviour made me hesitant to disclose anything to him.

Little did I know that this detective, named Peter, was involved in a web of infidelity. He was engaged to a pregnant woman, despite already being married. Fate had a twisted sense of humour when the woman he was engaged to and another pregnant woman coincidentally shared adjacent hospital beds. Both women discovered their boyfriends were policemen and named Peter, and upon sharing this shocking revelation, realized they were involved with the same deceitful detective. It was an unimaginable tale of betrayal and deception.

Upon learning of Peter's actions, one of the women's brothers took swift action and reported him to the Chief Superintendent, Mr. Jackson. Outraged by the revelation, Mr. Jackson stormed out of his office, seeking out Peter. Without hesitation, he terminated his employment on the spot. Such swift justice was unheard of in those days. Peter went on to marry one of the pregnant women, whose father happened to be a prosperous butcher. With his father-in-law's assistance, Peter established a taxi firm.

This astonishing account leaves one questioning the true nature of individuals, as even the most seemingly upstanding and educated can possess hidden vices. It serves as a stark reminder that one cannot judge a book by its cover, and that trust and integrity can be shattered in the most unexpected ways.

CHAPTER THIRTY-EIGHT

DISTRESS AND HUMILIATION AND THE POLICE OFFICERS WIFE

During my acquaintance with a police officer's wife, she confided in me about a distressing incident involving her husband and his drunken behaviour. She revealed that on occasions when he was heavily intoxicated, he would inadvertently urinate on her while she was asleep in bed. The following day, he would feel immense embarrassment upon realizing his actions, unaware of his state during the incident. She drew a comparison to animals marking their territory, illustrating the nature of the behaviour. She entrusted me with this information, urging me to maintain confidentiality and not disclose it to others. The thought of such an invasive and humiliating act brought forth empathy for the individual who had endured this violation of personal boundaries.

The impact of such an incident on a person's emotional well-being and sense of safety is difficult to comprehend. The violation of trust and the invasion of personal space in such a vulnerable state is deeply unsettling. The mere contemplation of experiencing such an act invokes a mixture of disbelief and sympathy for the individual affected.

Amidst these anecdotes, they faced a tumultuous journey that ultimately led to their divorce. The dissolution of their marriage carried a heavy weight of sadness, as it marked the end of what was once a promising union.

CHAPTER THIRTY-NINE

SHOPLIFTING SHENANIGANS

Ah, the tale of the notorious shoplifter in Kirkby. I recall the time when a detective at the station caught a woman red-handed and assigned me the task of searching her house. Low and behold, her humble abode was overflowing with stolen goodies, ranging from household items to clothes and even furniture. She was in the process of moving out, eagerly awaiting her new council house in the budding town of Kirkby. Our duty was to repossess all the pilfered treasures, and we returned them to the Bon Marche store, which was quite large. As a token of appreciation, they allowed me to choose anything I wanted from their clothing section. Ah, that beige suit I snagged was a gem, worth a whopping £300 back then! It was a straight skirt, three-quarter jacket business suit, and I cherished it for a good 15 years. Of course, I had to seek permission from work to accept such a gift, and thankfully, the sergeant gave the go-ahead. Oh, the perks of the job!

I will never forget the woman's cunning plan to acquire a fabulous three-piece suite for her bedroom. It had a lovely green marquee colour. She must have been quite determined because she managed to trick the shop by having two individuals dressed as workmen walk in and claim they were delivering the suite. Nonchalantly, they picked it up and strolled out, with everyone assuming they were legitimate. That house was a treasure trove of goods. I suppose she was quite resourceful, making sure that when she moved into her brand-new council house, everything would be fresh and delightful.

CHAPTER FORTY

UNVEILING THE NUISANCE CALLER: A SHOCKING TALE OF DECEPTION AND CONSEQUENCES

Another case was an investigation into a fellow who began causing trouble for an innocent woman. It all started with a simple telephone call, where he pretended to have dialled the wrong number. However, this was only the beginning of his tormenting antics. On another occasion, he called again, engaging the woman in a conversation that could only be described as a nuisance. Sensing something amiss, the woman's husband grew suspicious and urged her to involve the authorities. Responding to her plea, I, a dedicated police officer, paid her a visit for an interview. She shared her ordeal, recounting the persistent nuisance calls she had been receiving. Determined to resolve the matter, I assured her that I would take care of it.

With a plan in mind, I decided to take matters into my own hands (with agreement from the sergeant). I meticulously dressed up, contemplating a rendezvous at the corner near the local police station. It seemed like the perfect spot to confront the mysterious caller. As I reached the designated meeting point, a man pulled up alongside me, rolling down his window to greet me in a friendly manner. Seizing the opportunity, I calmly requested that he drive into the police station, intending for him to turn around afterwards. Agreeing without suspicion, he complied with my request.

Upon reaching the police station, I revealed my true identity, declaring myself a police officer. The unsuspecting man, who turned out to be a magistrate from the neighbouring town of Ormskirk, near Kirkby, was left shocked and apprehended for his actions. As news of his arrest spread, it soon reached the ears of the court. Recognizing his name on the court's list, someone realized his identity, prompting an influx of press coverage. The media seized the opportunity, creating a widespread exposé that unmasked the magistrate. The consequences were severe, as he was forced to step down from his council position. The relentless scrutiny and public backlash that followed mercilessly tore apart his reputation.

Regrettably, this turn of events also took a toll on his unsuspecting wife, who had remained oblivious to her husband's unsettling behaviour. In today's context, such actions could be categorized as stalking. Unaware of the man's family background or personal circumstances, I arrived at the court solely armed with the list of distressing telephone calls he had made to the tormented woman. It was a situation that spiralled into a tragic outcome, leaving lasting consequences for all involved.

CHAPTER FORTY-ONE

KIRKBY AND FAMILY LIFE FOR THE LANCASHIRE FOLK

W ithin the town of Kirkby, there resided a lovely family known as the Peters. Mr. and Mrs. Peters were the proud parents of six lively and spirited boys. Although they carried a reputation for their rough demeanour, their love for their children shone through in every interaction. Each of their sons possessed a striking handsomeness, reflecting the unique blend of their parents' traits. Memories of the Peters family flood my mind, and one particular incident stands out.

On that day, as I observed the bustling household, my attention was drawn to Mrs. Peters, gracefully nurturing the youngest member of the family. With one baby cradled in her arms, she skillfully switched to another bottle, containing a dark brown liquid, to the baby's lips.

I couldn't resist asking about this unconventional practice. "What are you giving the baby?" I inquired, genuinely intrigued.

With a warm smile, Mrs. Peters enlightened me about her ingenious technique. She revealed that she had prepared a stew for the family, and had taken some of the savoury gravy into the bottle. By doing so, she aimed to provide additional nutrients and expose her children to a variety of Flavors from an early age. It was an inventive and resourceful approach, a testament to her unwavering dedication as a mother

Despite their mischievous tendencies, the Peters boys were far from being truly wayward. They possessed a spirited nature, yet their hearts were pure and kind. As they grew, it became evident that they were not just mischievous lads but also robust and healthy individuals, a testament to their upbringing and the care they received within their nurturing home.

Chapter Forty-Two

Navigating Family Concerns and Media Attention

I once had to deal with a rape case. The story erupted, capturing the attention of both the public and the infamous News of the World. And there it was, in black and white, my name splashed across the pages. The news travelled quickly, reaching even the ears of my concerned mother. In a state of worry, she implored me to give up my job, firmly believing that I hadn't been raised to handle such harrowing cases.

My mother was afraid that news would reach Mayo in western Ireland where my mother hailed from. The News of the World was banned in Ireland due to its provocative nature.

It was then that I realized my resourceful mother had for many years concocted a scheme to send the newspaper in disguise by placing it within the pages of the Catholic Universe, a publication more widely accepted in Ireland. In her eyes, this clever ruse would ensure that the relatives in the West of Ireland, where she hailed from could receive the weekly news from England.

The situation was lost on me. Here I was, being urged to abandon my career, while my mother herself was stealthily sending supposedly provocative newspapers disguised within a catholic newspaper. The humorous contradiction of her actions amidst her concerns left me both astounded and amused.

Chapter Forty-Three

JURY ROOM AND COURT ANTICS

I was a rookie cop fresh-faced and naive on session duty one day, I couldn't believe my eyes when PC Black, the odd but humorous police officer, decided to waltz into the jury room instead of dutifully standing guard outside. It was as if he had a sixth sense for anarchy, and that day, confusion was exactly what he brought to the courtroom.

The trial had been proceeding smoothly, with lawyers presenting their cases and witnesses testifying. The atmosphere in the courtroom was tense, as everyone awaited the jury's decision. Little did we know, PC Black had other plans that would turn this ordinary trial into a memorable event.

As the jury retired to their secluded room to deliberate the case, PC Black, with a naughty twinkle in his eye, quietly followed them in. None of us, including the presiding judge, had any idea what he was up to. As the door closed behind him, the courtroom fell into a peculiar silence.

A few minutes later, the confusion began to spread like wildfire. The judge looked puzzled, the lawyers exchanged bemused glances, and the participants whispered amongst themselves. "Where on earth is PC Black?" was the question on everyone's mind. It was an unprecedented situation, and nobody knew how to handle it.

Curiosity finally got the better of us, and a few brave individuals, including myself, approached the jury room door. We were hesitant to disturb the sanctity of the jury's deliberations, but the mystery was just too compelling. With trepidation, we knocked gently on the door.

To our astonishment, there he was, PC Black, casually seated among the jurors, engaged in animated conversation. Not a single person in that room had any inkling that he was a police officer. He had blended seamlessly into the group, sharing jokes and stories as if he were an old friend.

The scene was surreal, and we were all left dumbfounded. The trial had to be promptly cancelled as it was impossible to maintain the impartiality and integrity of the jury with PC Black in their midst. The judge had no choice but to declare a mistrial, and the courtroom was abuzz with bewilderment.

As PC Black emerged from the jury room, his quirky grin remained firmly in place. He had managed to turn a routine day in court into a memorable spectacle. While the trial might have been cancelled, the legend of PC Black's unconventional humour lived on, and his reputation as the most unpredictable and amusing officer in the force was cemented that day.

Though we never truly understood why he chose to infiltrate the jury room, one thing was certain: PC Black had an uncanny ability to bring laughter and chaos wherever he went, leaving us all with a story we would retell for years to come.

CHAPTER FORTY-FOUR

THE LONELY BACHELOR AND THE TROUBLING INCIDENT

I remember an incident with regards to a gentleman residing in an apartment block, whose life took an unexpected turn when an incident was reported to the police, leading to an investigation that culminated in his arrest. This man, a bachelor in his late 50s, led a solitary life with limited social connections. Neighbours became suspicious when they noticed two young girls, aged 14 and 15, frequently visiting his flat.

As part of my police duties, it fell upon me to take a statement from the man involved. During the interview, he admitted to engaging in inappropriate behaviour. Specifically, he confessed to touching the boobs of the young girls, as a reward he would secretly give them money. Surprisingly, upon interviewing the girls, they confirmed the man's actions, stating that they were not harmed in any way and didn't mind the situation as they received money from him. The man seemed to believe his actions were innocent, perhaps influenced by the girls' perceived maturity compared to his own.

Given the circumstances and evidence collected during the investigation, I had no choice but to charge him with a charge indecent assault. The legal process required me to take an official statement from the man. During the statement-taking process, he unexpectedly divulged a personal concern about his appearance, specifically mentioning that he believed he had big ears. He requested that this detail be included in the statement, believing it might somehow assist his case.

The matter proceeded to court, where a particular judge presided over the proceedings. This judge was known for a peculiar habit; whenever something amusing was mentioned during the trial, he would lean forward, touch his wig, and flip it forward over his forehead. As I stood before the court, reading out the statement, the judge's distinctive wig-flipping gesture evoked amusement, causing me to stifle my laughter, and the jury's faces also revealed smirks.

Ultimately, the man was found guilty and received a six-month prison sentence. In a somewhat lighthearted remark during the sentencing, the judge referred to the man's earlier concern about his ears, suggesting that during his time away, he might consider seeking assistance for his self-perceived issue.

CHAPTER FORTY-FIVE

LANCASHIRE'S PIONEERING POLICE WOMEN: PATROLLING IN SPORTS CARS

C olonel Sir Eric St Johnston, the esteemed Chief Constable of Lancashire Con-
stabulary. In 1959, Colonel Johnston introduced a pioneering initiative called the
'Crime Cars. This system revolutionized police patrolling by enabling beat officers to cover a
significantly wider area efficiently. The Seaforth Crime Patrol, for instance, adopted the use
of a Ford Zephyr, enhancing their mobility and effectiveness in tackling criminal activities.

In the late 1950s, Lancashire stood as one of the country's largest police forces outside of
London, gaining a reputation for pioneering innovations in highway policing. From adopt-

ing radar technology to their selection of patrol cars, they were at the forefront of progress. Among their fleet, the MGs also played a significant role, as they were commissioned as early as 1932, and the sleek A roadster joined their ranks in late 1955.

With a focus on maximizing the MG's visibility, patrols were conducted with the hood lowered, adding to the car's distinctive profile. Yet, despite the allure of these vehicles, being on duty during severe winters posed undeniable challenges to the officers.

The MGs were equipped with a Pye transmitter, taking up much of the boot space. In addition to this, a specialized Traffic Car was necessary to carry essential equipment such as white coats, flares, "Accident" signs, hurricane lamps, fire extinguishers, first aid kits, and "incident" boxes. This array of equipment, while essential, left no room for a spare tyre in the MGs, should a tyre blow-out occur during a patrol, officers had to radio for a Ford Zephyr to bring a replacement wheel.

Lancashire's highway police, with their distinctive MG patrols, played a vital role in maintaining road safety and order. Their innovative approach to highway policing and their fleet of MGs marked a significant period in the region's law enforcement history. Despite the challenges and limitations, they faced, their dedication to keeping the roads safe is a testament to their commitment and professionalism.

Chief Constable Johnston believed that women who were trained as traffic officers should have the privilege of driving sports cars. It was a pioneering move that garnered attention and made headlines.

Traditionally, police vehicles were not associated with sports cars or painted in white. However, Mr. Johnston sought to challenge conventions and provide women with the opportunity to patrol in style. The traffic cars were exclusively designated for women officers, and their white paint made them stand out amidst the sea of traditional police vehicles.

One of the notable women officers to join the traffic unit was Joanne, a tall and skilled driver. She took to driving the sports cars with enthusiasm, becoming one of the few women in the force to operate these eye-catching vehicles.

The Lancashire County Force's innovative approach to policing caught the attention of the media. An article in the Telegraph highlighted the fleet of MG sports cars being used by the county's female officers. It was written in admiration of their speed, stating that these women were "fast." The MG sports cars had the capability to reach speeds of up to 100 miles per hour, a remarkable feat for police vehicles at that time.

To further distinguish the traffic officers, the sports cars were equipped with two-tone klaxon horns, and with a bell. The white uniform caps worn by these officers added to their unique appearance.

However, these sports cars did come with some challenges. They lacked heaters, which meant that during cold weather, the officers had to bundle up with blankets over their legs to keep warm.

Chief Johnston's initiative proved to be a significant step in promoting women's presence in law enforcement and challenging gender norms. The distinctive sight of policewomen driving white sports car convertibles became a symbol of progress and modernity in the Lancashire County Force.

The success of this initiative extended beyond the UK, as the idea of policewomen driving sports cars made its way to America. Mr. Johnston's vision of having policewomen patrol in style and gaining positive publicity for the force achieved international recognition.

As I reflect on this chapter in history, I am reminded of the courage and determination of those trailblazing women who drove the sports cars, breaking barriers and paving the way for future generations of female officers in law enforcement. Their legacy continues to inspire and demonstrate the potential for innovation and progress within the police force.

Chapter Forty-Six

KIRKBY STATION AND Z CARS - MISTAKEN IDENTITY AMIDST A POLICE SCENE

In January 1962, the British Broadcasting Corporation (BBC) launched a groundbreaking police drama series that would go on to captivate audiences across the nation. Titled "Z Cars," the show took viewers on thrilling adventures, following two unmarked Zephyr Mk. IIs as they patrolled the fictional town of Newtown in Lancashire, the North West of England. *Z Cars* as an idea came to creator Troy Ken. Building upon the success and principles of the 'Crime Cars project', "Z Cars" brought authenticity to the screen by featuring genuine squad cars. In the inaugural series, Ford GB generously provided the formidable Zephyr 6 Mk. IIIs, setting the stage for subsequent thrilling episodes that would keep audiences on the edge of their seats.

As the show's popularity surged, "Z Cars" would not only become a television sensation but also a significant influence on future police procedural dramas. Its legacy would endure through the years, leaving an indelible mark on the landscape of crime television and forever remembered as a pioneer in the genre.

In an unexpected turn of events, I found myself immersed in a bewildering situation. Returning from my duty in the CID car, I was met with a scene filled with policemen and police cars outside. Unbeknownst to me at the time, they were all actors, engaged in a theatrical production. The commotion left me without any available parking space, adding to the confusion of the moment.

Amidst the chaos, a kind-hearted individual noticed my predicament and graciously offered to move his car, creating a much-needed space for me. Little did I know that this individual was also part of the production, taking on the role of a police officer.

During the days when Z Cars was being filmed, the scriptwriters would come up to Kirkby, and I would often have lunch with one of them. They didn't want to delve into the intricate details of specific cases but rather sought a general understanding of police work. However, when I eventually watched Z Cars on television, I couldn't help but notice that none of the episodes seemed to reflect any particular crime I was familiar with. Nevertheless, they did bring a police dog on set. Now, police dogs are typically well-behaved around officers, but this one was a real troublemaker. His name was Jasper, and he would go after anyone who dared enter the police dog office. Stepping into that office unprepared meant risking a sudden jump and a potential throat encounter. That Jasper was quite the character!

Chapter Forty-Seven

Revelry and Rivalry: Off-Duty Police Officer Antics in 1950s Lancashire, England

O ff-duty police officers often frequented local pubs to unwind and share laughs with their colleagues. Drinking games like darts, shove ha'penny, and dominoes were popular pastimes that fostered friendly competition and camaraderie. These games allowed officers to let their hair down, share stories and create lasting memories over a pint or two.

Gambling was another prevalent off-duty activity among police officers. They engaged in friendly wagers on various events, from horseracing to local football matches. Poker nights were common, and officers showcased their poker faces while enjoying each other's company. The stakes were often kept low, focusing more on the thrill of the game and friendly banter than on monetary gains.

Football was a passion for many in Lancashire, and off-duty police officers were no exception. Engaging in casual matches at local fields, they formed their teams, donning their kits with pride. These games were a source of friendly rivalry between different precincts, with good-natured banter and jests exchanged before, during, and after the matches.

Beyond their interdepartmental competitions, off-duty police officers embraced community engagement through charity football events. Participating in matches to raise funds for local causes, they showcased their skills on the field while fostering a strong bond with the communities they served.

While indulging in these antics, off-duty police officers never lost sight of their duty and commitment to the community. Even in their recreational activities, the spirit of unity and service prevailed. They continued to carry themselves with the same sense of responsibility and integrity that defined their profession.

The camaraderie fostered through these antics extended far beyond the precinct. Off-duty police officers developed a genuine sense of brotherhood, forming friendships that transcended their professional lives. This close-knit bond played a crucial role in building a strong and reliable police force, united in both duty and leisure.

The antics and recreational activities of off-duty police officers in 1950s Lancashire left a lasting legacy. They showcased the human side of these law enforcers, emphasizing that behind the badge were individuals who appreciated moments of relaxation and camaraderie. The sense of unity and commitment to their community, even in their leisure, epitomized the dedication that made these officers a pillar of trust and protection for the people of Lancashire.

The antics of off-duty police officers in 1950s Lancashire provided a window into their social lives and the sense of camaraderie that defined their profession. These officers fostered a strong bond of friendship and unity that extended beyond their precincts. Amidst the laughter and friendly rivalries, they continued to carry the spirit of service and dedication that defined their roles as protectors of the community. These off-duty escapades showcased the human side of the police force, reminding us that behind the uniform, they were individuals who embraced moments of camaraderie, joy, and community engagement. The next chapter refers to some of those antics....

CHAPTER FORTY-EIGHT

HILARIOUS HIJINKS: A POLICE CONFERENCE TALE

During my time in the police force, attending conferences was both a professional and social affair. Male and female officers would come together to learn and bond, often staying overnight at hotels. Now, these events were supposed to be serious, but let me tell you, some of the antics the lads got up to were unbelievable!

One particular conference took place in the heart of Liverpool City Centre, and as regulars at such events, we decided to book into a familiar B&B. We knew the owners and staff well, and they were used to our rowdy group making appearances.

After a night out on the town with copious amounts of alcohol consumed, the lads decided it was time to call it a night. Four of them were sharing a room, and that's when the mischief began. One officer was in a particularly bad state and urgently needed to relieve himself. Little did he know that his fellow officers had hatched a diabolical plan involving cling film!

Under the cover of darkness, they meticulously covered the toilet seat with cellophane cling film and put the seat back down to conceal their prank. The unsuspecting officer rushed into the bathroom, desperate to answer nature's call. He lifted the lid and, due to his pressing urgency, unleashed a mighty stream of urine. But it wasn't a typical bathroom experience for him.

The cling film redirected his stream, causing his pee to splash back all over his face, clothes, the ceiling, and the floor. Can you imagine his astonishment? Meanwhile, the other officers, safely tucked away in their room, couldn't contain their laughter at the unfolding spectacle.

The next day, they returned to the station, only to find out that the B&B owner had filed a complaint. Despite their efforts to clean up the mess, the unmistakable aroma of pee lingered in the room. As a punishment, the officers involved had two weeks' pay deducted from their salaries, to pay for special cleaning of the room. You'd think that would deter them, right? Oh no, the shenanigans continued every time they attended a conference!

Now, as lady officers, we remained blissfully unaware of the wild events of the previous evening. Frankly, I don't think female officers would even conceive of such antics! Our conferences were likely filled with far fewer outrageous moments and much more sensible discussions.

So, there you have it – a true tale from my time in the police force, where even the most serious of conferences could turn into hilariously unforgettable experiences. And while some officers had to learn their lessons the hard way, I can assure you that our gatherings were never short on laughter and camaraderie.

Chapter Forty-Nine

(MORCAMBE) ADVENTURES OF THE POLICE FORCE

Within the headquarters, amusing stories circulated about the off-duty police officers who regularly embarked on weekend getaways to the picturesque town of Morecambe. Nestled in Morecambe was a large beautiful park featuring a charming bandstand, which became the chosen resting spot for these adventurous officers armed with their trusty sleeping bags.

As the evening rolled in, their escapades began, and the officers soon struck up a friendship with a local bar owner who had a penchant for importing cider from down South. This cider might have been on the cheaper side, but it certainly left much to be desired in the refreshment department its rather bitter taste left no doubt about that!

Now, prepare yourself for the good-natured mischief that took place during one memorable gathering. These brave officers decided to challenge each other to a drinking competition, testing their mettle with the imported cider. Laughter filled the air as the contest ensued, and it wasn't long before the first contestant surrendered, admitting defeat with a grin.

Not to be outdone, they then engaged in an arm-wrestling contest, with much bravado and banter. Strong arms clashed, and amidst the playful groans and cheers, a true champion emerged, claiming bragging rights until the next gathering.

But the fun didn't end there. Card games were a staple of these off-duty shenanigans, and the officers revelled in friendly and competitive matches. The stakes might have been small, but the camaraderie and laughter were immeasurable.

One officer, perhaps a little too tipsy for his good, thought it wise to create a concoction of tea bags and Fairy Liquid. In his slightly inebriated state, he believed he was being clever and amusing, but let's just say it was more on the idiotic side. Unable to muster the courage to swallow the bizarre mixture, he had no choice but to spit it out in a less-than-dignified manner, leading to uproarious laughter from his fellow officers.

But fear not, the local bobbies on the beat, familiar with these boisterous officers, kept a watchful eye to ensure they caused no trouble. While they checked in on them, they knew better than to interfere, understanding that sometimes good-natured antics could lead to lasting memories and legendary stories.

The Morecambe adventures of these police officers were a delightful blend of camaraderie, laughter, and occasional stomach-churning challenges. Amidst the merriment and seemingly ludicrous escapades, lifelong friendships were forged, and bonds were strengthened. And though some of the tales might have raised a few eyebrows, they became part of the cherished folklore that brought smiles to the faces of those who knew the officers involved. These spirited getaways were a testament to the playful spirit and close-knit bonds shared by the dedicated members of the police force.

CHAPTER FIFTY

FROM POLICEWOMAN TO THE SCRAP TRADE: HILARIOUS TALES OF BUSES AND GYPSIES"

A this point in my life, I was married and had my daughter Lucy. I found myself facing the challenge of shift work, which unfortunately limited the amount of time I could spend with Lucy, as I desired. Recognizing the need for a job offering greater flexibility, I decided to explore the realm of the scrap trade. It all began when I spotted an advertisement in the local paper seeking a man to run an office. Well, I couldn't resist challenging their assumption that only a man could handle the job. I wrote them a letter, stating that I was as capable as any man to run an office. To my surprise, I met the person in a pub. When I asked what the job entailed, he hesitantly replied, "I'm a scrap merchant." I thought to myself, "Well, that's all I need!" But with a sense of adventure, I decided to give it a go and started working for them. It turned out that he was an honest man and a fantastic boss.

In the office, I was assigned to the buying department, which involved managing a big weighbridge station and purchasing scrap from the local gypsies. Let me tell you about one of the funniest incidents that took place during my time there. One fine morning, a gentleman named Barry strolled into the office and asked if we would buy a bus. I agreed but made it clear that I would deduct half the weight for anything inside the bus that couldn't be used for scrap, such as seats.

Later that morning, as I glanced out of the office window, I noticed something peculiar. There, coming down the hill outside the yard, was Barry driving the bus. And behind him, with its lights flashing, was a police car! I thought to myself, "Hold on a minute, that's not scrap—it's a brand-new bus!" Barry had stolen it from the Reading bus depot! I quickly called my boss, and he came out to see what the commotion was all about. To my surprise, Barry turned to me and said, "Well, you did say if he brought a bus in, you would buy it!" The police promptly arrested Barry, but there was a slight dilemma—how were we supposed to continue our operations with a stolen bus sitting on the weighbridge? We had a queue of customers waiting for hours to get in, as we were always incredibly busy, buying hundreds of tons of scrap every day. Eventually, someone from the Reading bus depot arrived and moved the bus off the weighbridge.

As fate would have it, the gypsy who had visited us earlier still believed it was acceptable to swipe a bus. I couldn't help but confront him, saying, "When I said I would buy a bus, I didn't expect you to go and steal one!" His defence? "Well, they shouldn't have left the keys in it!" Oh, the antics of the scrap trade never cease to amaze.

CHAPTER FIFTY-ONE

THE GYPSY FAMILIES: CULINARY DELIGHTS AND SURPRISING WEDDING STORIES

During my time working at the yard, I formed close bonds with several gypsy families who frequented the place. They were such welcoming people that they often invited me over for meals, and let me tell you, some of them were exceptional cooks! Talk about a luxurious experience—there was one family who had shelves adorned with stunning crystal pieces. The father, a meticulous man, kept receipts for each crystal item, proudly displaying a collection worth over £20,000!

Their living arrangements were fascinating as well. They had three trailers—one served as the main gathering place where we shared meals, another was the sleeping quarters for the parents, and the third accommodated their six lively boys. It was clear that they were not lacking in wealth.

Now, let me regale you with a tale from one of the gypsy weddings I had the pleasure of attending. This particular wedding was for a gentleman named Paddy. After the ceremony, as we stepped outside, his brother Sean approached me, a mischievous glint in his eyes. He whispered, "There might be some trouble here. Paddy didn't use his own surname on the wedding certificate." Shocked and intrigued, I couldn't help but ask Sean why Paddy made such an unusual choice. With a smirk, he revealed the truth. "Well," he chuckled, "he doesn't particularly fancy her. She's been chasing after him for years, you see. He figured if he married her, she'd finally leave him alone. It's a wild solution, isn't it?" Oh, the lengths people go to to avoid persistent admirers!

CHAPTER FIFTY-TWO

THE GENEROUS BOSS, JAMAICAN GETAWAYS, AND AN UNEXPECTED BANK ENCOUNTER

I was fortunate to have a boss who was not only good but also incredibly generous. Every Christmas, he would bless me with a substantial bonus, usually around £5,000. My daughter Lucy and I made it a tradition to indulge ourselves with a luxurious two-week vacation at a top hotel in Jamaica, thanks to these generous bonuses.

In our yard, we had a sizable refrigerator, and we came up with a brilliant idea to sell crisps and coke. It turned out to be a roaring success, as there were times when the queue at the weighbridge stretched on for two hours. We earned quite a tidy profit from this venture. However, we eventually decided to sell the house and relocate, setting our sights on a new home. To secure a deposit for the new house while waiting for ours to sell, I approached the bank, seeking a loan of £10,000.

To my surprise, I received an urgent phone call from the bank manager, requesting an immediate meeting. My mind raced with thoughts of house security checks and various formalities. Little did I know that the reason for the urgency was entirely different. During our conversation, the manager raised a rather unexpected concern. He questioned how I supported myself since he noticed that I rarely withdrew any money from the bank. In response, I candidly explained our successful sideline of selling crisps and coke from the fridge in the yard. The manager's response left me momentarily startled—he warned me about the potential trouble if the taxman were to uncover our business. It dawned on me that our profits from the venture had effectively replaced the need for drawing regular wages from the bank. It was a realization I had never pondered before. From that point on, I made sure to regularly withdraw money from the bank to avoid any further scrutiny.

Such encounters remind us of the unexpected twists and turns life can bring, even when we think we're simply finding creative solutions to support ourselves.

CHAPTER FIFTY-THREE

THE GYPSY CONFERENCE ENCOUNTER AND RISE TO MANAGING DIRECTOR

When the staff from the yard attended a conference, I found myself in London, having just exited Simpsons the shoe shop. Lost in my thoughts, I glanced up and noticed a person walking towards me. Our eyes met, and we exchanged smiles. What caught my attention was the exquisite Vancouver coat he was wearing. It was a luxurious garment made from a special material, favoured by wealthy gypsies. Curiously, I asked if he was heading to the conference. He seemed puzzled by my assumption and inquired about the reason behind it. I explained that his coat was reminiscent of what the affluent gypsies often wore. However, it soon became apparent that I had mistaken him for someone else. With a bemused expression I exclaimed, "Ah, I recognize you now. You're Anthony Quinn, the actor." , It was true that in his younger days, Anthony Quinn had a certain resemblance to a gypsy. He chuckled, never expecting to be labelled a wealthy gypsy on the streets of London. "I'll cherish this story forever," he said. "In America, nobody will believe that I was mistaken for a gypsy in London." He then asked if I recognized him, to which I replied affirmatively yes, though not as a film star. I had genuinely thought he was a gypsy. He playfully requested, "Stop calling me a gypsy!" In our conversation, he asked about my occupation, and I mentioned that I worked in the scrap trade.

Later, he extended a gracious invitation for me to join him and his wife for coffee at the Ritz. Regrettably, I had to decline as I was the only woman attending the conference, and I needed to be present. As I've learned, gypsies could become somewhat displeased if you couldn't recall their names.

Meanwhile, the owner of the scrap yard recognized my capabilities and appointed me as the managing director. He was not only a good man but also a genuinely pleasant individual. His father held him in high regard and even bought him some land, which contributed to the tremendous success of our business.

This encounter with Anthony Quinn, coupled with my professional advancement, added some delightful twists to my journey in the scrap trade.

CHAPTER FIFTY-FOUR

EDUCATION WITHIN THE GYPSY COMMUNITY

Within the cohort of Gypsy individuals who graced the yard, a notable presence emerged in the form of a barrister. His unique journey set him apart from the norm of his Gypsy contemporaries during that era. Unlike many within the Gypsy community, children were often pulled out of formal education at the tender age of 12 to contribute to their family's business endeavours, this individual was afforded the opportunity to pursue his education.

His triumph was not just a personal achievement, but a testament to the potential that lies within the Gypsy community when provided with the chance to explore their aspirations.

His success serves as a shining example that dispels any misconception about the Gypsy community's limitations.

During this period, another individual named Callum, hailing from the Gypsy community, entered the scrap yard. Callum was the only child in his family and hadn't acquired the skill of reading or writing. Despite this, he was the proud father of a nine-year-old daughter. Every Saturday, he would take his daughter to Smith's Book Shop, purchasing two books for her.

On a particular occasion, Callum broached the subject of needing to visit his daughter's school. Out of curiosity, I inquired as to the reason, eager to learn about the situation. Callum's response revealed that the school had acknowledged his daughter's remarkable intelligence and had proposed that she attend a special school tailored to her needs.

Following these incidents, the local library initiated reading lessons for the general public, which attracted the attention of many Gypsies. They eagerly seized the opportunity to learn how to read and write. Previously, such education was not commonplace within their community.

Notably, there was another Gypsy family whose teenage son constantly found himself in trouble. Faced with the challenge of keeping him out of trouble, the police decided to send him to an approved school when he was 14 or 15 years old. The boy remained there for three years, a period during which approved schools were transitioning to community orders as a form of punishment. When the young man completed his time at the school, a remarkable transformation had taken place. He established his own business, specializing in tarmacking roads, and even employed a team of seven individuals. The impact of his time in the approved school was undeniable.

Callum's story and the experiences of these Gypsies shed light on the evolving attitudes towards education within their community. The recognition of a child's intelligence and the subsequent push for specialized schooling indicated a shift in priorities. Moreover, the transformation of the troubled teenager, who found success after his time in an approved school, exemplified the positive influence that structured education and rehabilitative programs can have on individuals.

This highlights the importance of education and the opportunities it can provide, even within traditionally marginalized communities. The journey of Callum and the Gypsies serves as a testament to the power of learning and personal growth, ultimately paving the way for a brighter future within their community.

CHAPTER FIFTY-FIVE

A POLICEWOMAN'S JOURNEY OF LOVE: HARRY'S FIRST DATE: A MEMORABLE ENCOUNTER

Earlier in my life, I had a few boyfriends before I met my husband, but they didn't captivate my interest. During my time in the police force, I once dated a rather wealthy man I met at a nightclub. He owned a luxurious Rolls Royce. On our third outing together, I noticed a large Elastoplast placed along his dashboard, covering the mileage indicator. Curious, I asked him about it, and he revealed that it was to prevent the police from knowing how many miles he had driven. He seemed worried that they might investigate his activities.

Our relationship ended abruptly after that incident, and it's quite possible that he obtained his Rolls Royce through dubious means.

During my service as a policewoman, I came into contact with a man named Harry. He was older than I and was in a separated marital state due to the complex divorce procedures of that time. My mother expressed disapproval of our relationship due to the situation. Harry held the rank of Major in the army although he had left the army at this time. Nevertheless, we decided to establish a home together in 1966, fully aware of the complexities we would face.

Years passed, and it wasn't until 1972 that divorce became more acceptable and feasible. The new laws allowed one party to proceed with a divorce if the other party refused to do so. Seizing this opportunity, Harry and I decided to marry.

Our journey navigated the complexities of societal norms and legal limitations. While faced with disapproval and obstacles, we found a way to overcome them and build a life together. The transformative shift in divorce laws played a crucial role in enabling us to take this significant step forward.

In this story of ours, I met a guy named Harry, though he liked being called Greg more. He didn't like it when I used his full name, Harold, especially when we were arguing. So, where did I first run into Greg? Well, he was in charge of a residential club in Kirkby. The way we met was pretty coincidental. Some of the folks from the police station would drop by the club for coffee, and they kept telling me to come meet the new manager. That's where we ended up crossing paths and getting to know each other.

For our first date, Greg took me to the Adelphi Hotel for dinner. I thought to myself, "I've hit the jackpot!" Unfortunately, the food turned out to be awful. I called the waiter and asked him to go into the kitchen, taste the food, and report back to me. He returned with an apology, admitting that the chef hadn't shown up that day and that the food was awful. As compensation, he offered us vouchers for a free meal another time. Greg was content to leave it at that, but I was famished. I asked can whoever is cooking able to do poached eggs on toast. He said yes, thank goodness. We received the vouchers by mail. When we finally returned to the hotel for another meal, it was delightful.

Another noteworthy aspect of that memorable evening was our attendance at the Liverpool Theatre to watch a performance by Marlene Dietrich. She sang the song "Lili Marlene" under the lamppost, and her presence was truly enchanting. Even though she was already considered older in 1964, she had a group of young admirers. It was no wonder she had such a devoted following. I had heard of her before, but witnessing her performance was something I would never forget. It was a truly fantastic night.

Regarding Greg, I considered him quite appealing and assumed he had some wealth, but that was not the case. However, he possessed a beautiful speaking voice, and I enjoyed listening to him whenever he spoke. He was a kind and pleasant person. At times, I would purposely try to astonish him, perhaps to embarrass him a little. Years later, he mentioned that he would never forget the incident at the Adelphi Hotel when I asked the waiter to taste the food and identify it. I intended to express my sarcasm because the food was truly terrible. The Adelphi Hotel was reputed to be the finest establishment in Liverpool and the entire northern region of England.

I chose to elope with my husband, Greg, to the Wandsworth register office to solemnize our union. As I was raised in the Catholic faith, marrying a divorced man posed a challenge since the Catholic Church did not allow such marriages. Therefore, we opted for a simple ceremony at the registry office, surrounded by Greg's sister and four close friends, making our marriage legal and official.

Unfortunately, my parents disapproved of our union due to the age difference and Greg's previous divorce, which led them to refrain from attending the wedding. Despite their reservations, we continued to maintain a connection with them, visiting them occasionally and welcoming them to our home.

CHAPTER FIFTY-SIX

A HILARIOUS STROLL WITH GREG AND THE GREAT DANES

G reg and I shared a delightful habit of taking leisurely walks together, accompanied by our two mischievous Great Danes. Our preferred route took us through a picturesque park and along a charming canal. However, one fateful day, the unexpected occurred—Greg lost his footing and tumbled into the canal. It was a sight to behold, and I couldn't contain my laughter, though I tried my best to stifle it. It proved to be quite a challenge!

With a mischievous grin, I enquired, "Are you very wet?" Greg, still dripping from his unexpected plunge, gave me a bemused look and replied, "Not really." It turned out that his elegant jacket had become adorned with an exquisite layer of algae, adding an unexpected touch to his attire.

As if that weren't enough, our misadventure continued when our mischievous dogs decided to wander off and explore. They had an affinity for rolling around in fox excrement, much to our dismay. The drive back home became a struggle, as the pungent odor filled the car. We had no choice but to roll down the windows, subjecting ourselves to the stench in the hope of mitigating the situation.

Upon arrival, Greg took on the arduous task of hosing down our mirthful, yet foul-smelling, companions. It was a memorable end to our eventful walk, where laughter, unexpected dips, and canine antics prevailed.

CHAPTER FIFTY-SEVEN

THE CASE OF THE MISSING CASH AND A DIPLOMATIC BOSS

I didn't go in to work until about 11:00 or 12:00 o'clock because I stayed later every night, I used to go through the daily tickets. I encountered a man with whom I had a transaction. Regrettably, I had inadvertently underpaid him due to a miscalculation on my part. Realizing my mistake the following day, I promptly prepared another ticket for him. During our interaction, I brought up the issue, admitting, "I believe I may have underpaid you yesterday. Did you have the chance to review your ticket?" To this, he responded, "I thought you had, but I encounter difficulties with reading and writing," he explained. He expressed his gratitude with a simple "Thank you." Surprisingly, the very next day, he presented me with a bottle of whiskey as a token of appreciation for my honesty. I had a bond of trust between myself and the gypsies as they thought I was married to a member of a famous gypsy family based in London.

It was just another ordinary night after a long day of work when my phone rang, and it was a call from the office. The voice on the other end informed me that there was an issue with the cash. Naturally, I asked, "How much is it off by?" In scenarios where it's a small amount, like £40 or £60, for instance, you know you may have misplaced your receipts but could trace it through the machine. The response hit me like a ton of bricks: "It's about £2,000!"

Without wasting any time, I hurried back to the office. Once there, a young woman and a coworker explained what had happened. She said, "I know exactly what went wrong. You see, today we withdrew the money from the bank, and most of it was in £20 notes, but I mistakenly counted them as £10 notes." This meant that someone had been overpaid by that significant amount. We narrowed down the suspects to two individuals—one of them was Seamus, a man who knew about our two unmarried sons. Although he didn't pay them a proper wage, he would provide them with pocket money. We had a hunch that he wouldn't inform us if we had accidentally overpaid him. The other person of interest was Aidan.

Amid this confusion, the boss arrived on the scene. The young woman promptly admitted her error to him. Sensing the delicate nature of the situation, the boss decided to handle it tactfully. He made a call to Aidan and straightforwardly asked if he had received the wrong amount of money. Aidan, being honest, replied, "If I had been given the wrong money, I would have called you immediately to let you know." Then came the moment to contact Seamus. The boss inquired if Seamus had opened his money yet. Seamus, pretending he hadn't already checked, responded, "No, but I'll go and verify it." Of course, the boss was aware that Seamus had indeed checked his money. Seamus eventually confessed, saying, "Oh yes, I've got your money."

Fortunately, we managed to retrieve the overpaid sum from Seamus. Otherwise, our trust in him would have been severely shaken, and we would have been hesitant to continue trading with him. It was a lesson learned, reminding us of the importance of careful attention to detail, and the diplomatic finesse exhibited by our boss in handling such delicate matters.

I vividly recall the time when my husband passed away. My surname is Gregory, which is associated with a gypsy heritage. One morning, as I parked my car outside the gates before heading to work, I stepped out of the vehicle. At that moment, one of the ladies I know from the scrapyard called out, expressing her condolences for my husband's loss. I replied, "It's alright." She proceeded to mention that my husband belonged to the London branch of the Gregory family, to which I affirmed with a "yes." She turned to her partner and said, "See, I was right. He was a Gregory." His name was Harry, and whilst he bore the surname of Gregory, he wasn't part of the gypsy community. Maybe, somewhere down the line, he had Irish heritage.

CHAPTER FIFTY-EIGHT

MEMOIRS OF WANDERLUST: ADVENTURES ACROSS CONTINENTS

Throughout the years, my husband Greg and I embarked on remarkable holidays to various exotic destinations, spanning Italy, Spain, Scotland, Ireland, Wales, Jamaica, and even the Maldives. One summer in Torremolinos, Greg surprised me with a property viewing. He was captivated by the idea of purchasing a beautiful house there for a mere £5000, which, considering it was five decades ago, was an incredible opportunity. However, my concerns for our daughter Lucy and her schooling held me back, as the concept of buying houses abroad was still relatively new at the time.

Despite the missed opportunity, our holidays were always delightful and filled with warm welcomes from the local people, especially in Spain. I recall the captivating architecture of Italy, such as the awe-inspiring Colosseum, and the moments we spent exploring places like the Vatican, absorbing history and culture.

One poignant memory finds us sitting in the Vatican square, where I read about the untimely passing of actor Richard Beckinsale in an English newspaper. It was a surreal moment, reading about such news in such a historic setting.

Our travels also took us on captivating coach tours, allowing us to explore numerous picturesque locations. One particular trip led us to the alluring island of Sicily. Fascinated by the tales of the Mafia, I kept my eyes peeled for any signs of their presence. Yet, as elusive as they were, we immersed ourselves in the beauty of Sicily, enjoying a lovely holiday despite my lingering curiosity.

As for our daughter Lucy, she embraced our travels with ease, although it was rather unusual for families to venture abroad during those times. For her, the experience of exploring different countries felt quite normal, and she cherished the adventures as if they were a natural part of life.

Looking back on our globetrotting experiences, I am filled with gratitude for the extraordinary memories we created as a family. Our escapades to far-off lands enriched our lives and broadened our horizons.

Chapter Fifty-Nine

Lost, Rain, and Unexpected Bites: An Unforgettable Holiday Adventure

In the year 1972, when long-distance travel was still quite unconventional, I embarked on a memorable vacation to the newly opened resort in the Maldives. Eager for exploration, one day we decided to embark on a long walk, driven by the allure of a rumoured secret beach. Oh, how we envisioned having the entire shoreline to ourselves!

As we embarked on our trek, our excitement grew with each step. Yet, despite our efforts, the elusive beach remained elusive. Undeterred, we continued our journey, hopeful that our perseverance would pay off. Little did we know that our adventure would take an unexpected turn.

Gradually, the sun began its descent, casting long shadows over our surroundings. Time seemed to slip away, and before we knew it, darkness engulfed us. It was as if a switch had been flipped, leaving us in pitch-black obscurity. Unable to see our own hands in front of us, panic started to set in.

Just when it seemed things couldn't get any worse, the heavens unleashed a torrential downpour. Rain poured from the sky as if cats and dogs were being showered upon us. It was a comical sight, drenched and disoriented in the middle of nowhere.

Thankfully, amidst the chaos, my quick-witted Gregory (Harry), spotted a large sewer pipe along our route. With limited options available, he suggested we seek shelter inside for the night. So, there we were, huddled in the unlikely refuge of a sewer pipe, trying to find solace in our predicament.

Yet, as if our misfortune wasn't already enough, fate had one more surprise in store for me. In the darkness, an unidentified creature decided to take a nibble on my unsuspecting toe. The pain and shock caused me to let out a shriek, forever leaving me perplexed about the peculiar intruder who had chosen my foot as a midnight snack.

With a mixture of humour and trepidation, our unexpected night spent in the sewer pipe became etched into our memories. The misplaced beach, the sudden darkness, the pouring rain, and the mysterious toe bite served as a reminder that even the most meticulously planned adventures can take whimsical turns.

The following morning, determined to return to the resort, we set out on our quest to find a bus. We trekked for what felt like ages, our tired bodies covered in dirt and sand, our once-neat hair now standing on end. It was an amusing sight, considering the other passengers at the bus stop were impeccably dressed or in neat uniforms. We couldn't help but feel a bit embarrassed by our dishevelled appearance.

As we stood in the queue, desperately awaiting our turn, we were met with curious glances and discreet chuckles from our fellow passengers. It was as if we were the main act in a comical circus, completely unaware of our starring roles. However, amidst the embarrassment, we clung to the hope of reaching the hotel, where food and drink awaited us after a whole day of deprivation.

Oh, the relief that washed over us when we finally arrived back at the resort! It felt like stepping into heaven itself. Exhausted, hungry, and parched, we eagerly made our way to the comfort of our room. The prospect of a shower became the beacon of respite after a challenging day.

With a sigh of contentment, we entered the shower, letting the warm water cascade over our weary bodies. The sand and grime were washed away, leaving behind a renewed sense of cleanliness and tranquillity. It was a moment of pure bliss, as the water cleansed not only our physical selves but also symbolized the cleansing of the chaotic events and unexpected misadventures of the previous day.

Chapter Sixty

JAMAICA: A TAPESTRY OF ADVENTURE, KINDNESS, AND RICH HISTORY

J amaica, a land of vibrant beauty, captivated my memories during our visits. One unforgettable excursion led us to Don's Rivers Falls, a magnificent cascade of water that enthralled our senses. As we ventured through the falls, I couldn't help but notice the slippery terrain and the forceful flow of water. Inevitably, I took a fall, but to my amazement, two caring Rastafarians, who were guiding us on the trip, swiftly came to my aid. Their kindness touched my heart as they ensured my well-being and tended to my slightly swollen ankle, diligently strapping it up for me.

r enchanting destination we explored was the Blue Hole, a mesmerizing turquoise
s nestled within the hills of Saint Mary's, alongside the White River. We revelled in
ing in the crystal-clear pools and delving into the mysteries of the nearby caves. The
ries created there remains a cherished treasure, each visit a testament to the immense
 of the surroundings. However, we learned that after heavy rainfall, the Blue Hole
ormed, as muddy and grassy banks formed due to the rushing rainwater carrying mud
tream. Following our invigorating swim, we would savour hot pumpkin soup and
e in the refreshing taste of coconut, both serving as delightful treats after our aquatic
tures.

naican cuisine captured my heart, particularly the flavoursome combination of chick-
e, and peas. A fellow officer at work, hailing from Jamaica, generously shared the recipe
me. Since then, I have continued to prepare this dish, receiving compliments from
ds who relish its taste.

he history of Jamaica also fascinated me. I discovered that the island's original inhabi-
ts, the Arawaks, arrived from South America approximately 2500 years ago. They named
he "land of wood and water" and cultivated crops such as cassava, sweet potatoes, and
rious fruits and vegetables. Eventually, the Spanish claimed Jamaica, followed by English
ale. However, in 1962, Jamaica gained independence from the United Kingdom, marking
a significant milestone in its history.

CHAPTER SIXTY-ONE

A JAMAICAN WEDDING ADVENTURE: RAIN, ROACHES, AND UNEXPECTED BLESSINGS

Our love for Jamaica was so profound that my daughter decided to tie the knot there in 1990. Little did we know that her wedding journey would be a story to remember. As soon as we stepped off the plane, a bold vendor approached us, attempting to sell cannabis. To our dismay, our suitcases were promptly searched, revealing the wedding dress, bridesmaid dress, and every secret we hoped to keep hidden. It was a rather humorous start to our Jamaican adventure.

Amidst the chaotic airport scene, a cheerful man in a rickety old char bang, worn-out bus—awaited us outside customs. Thunder roared, and lightning crackled as we embarked on a wild ride down winding roads at breakneck speed. The excitement mixed with unease as we reached our hotel, only to discover that a tropical storm had ravaged the area a few weeks prior. The unmistakable scent of dampness permeated everything. Our hotel room, unfortunately, was not exempt from unwelcome visitors, as cockroaches scurried about. My reaction was rather theatrical, jumping onto the bed and demanding their immediate removal.

Sunday marked our arrival, and Tuesday was set as the wedding day. The lady at the reception suggested a morning ceremony due to the impending tropical storms, but Lucy, my daughter, insisted on keeping the planned time of 2 p.m. On the morning of the wedding, however, a call from reception disrupted our preparations. It was only 11 o'clock, and the vicar had arrived. Lucy caught off guard, exclaimed, "I can't! I can't get married now. I'm not ready. You'll have to tell the vicar to come back later."

Despite the unexpected timing, the wedding proceeded as planned at 2 o'clock in the hotel lobby. What was supposed to be a serene ceremony in tropical gardens became a lively affair surrounded by the sound of storm and rain. Our attempts to capture the moment on tape proved futile as the elements drowned out the audio. However, the rain, thankfully, ceased after that day, and the rest of our time in Jamaica blessed us with glorious sunshine.

We stayed at the Shaw Park Beach Hotel, a charming colonial-style building situated right on the beach. The morning of the wedding held a precious memory as Lucy glanced outside and saw her husband and his best man on the jetty, enjoying a rain-free moment. She waved to them, basking in the anticipation of the day. To our delight, the waiter arrived with breakfast, offering reassurance amidst the wedding day jitters. He shared a heartwarming sentiment, "Don't worry about it raining on your wedding day, he said to Lucy, it's a sign of good luck I got married on a rainy day, and I've been married for 20 years." His kind words brought comfort and added sweetness to the occasion.

Amidst rain, roaches, and unforeseen blessings, Lucy's Jamaican wedding adventure became a testament to the unpredictability of life and the joy that can be found in embracing the unexpected. It remains a cherished tale, forever etched in our memories, reminding us of the unique and humorous moments that make life's journeys truly unforgettable.

Jamaica, a tapestry woven with adventure, acts of kindness, and a rich historical background, forever holds a special place in my heart. Its captivating beauty, warm-hearted people, and tantalizing flavours continue to evoke cherished memories and a sense of deep appreciation for the island's remarkable heritage.

CHAPTER SIXTY-TWO

LUCY'S MULTILEVEL GARDEN OASIS

In Lucy's charming garden, various levels add depth and character to the landscape. Upon stepping out of the front door, visitors are greeted by a well-maintained gravelled area. Ascending a few steps, one arrives at a cosy seating spot thoughtfully arranged by Lucy herself. Here, decorative baskets brimming with bird food hang gracefully, beckoning feathered friends to partake in the offering.

One day, while tending to her avian guests, Lucy spotted a peculiar sight. A lone bird lay motionless on the ground, seemingly in distress. Concerned for the little creature's well-being, she approached cautiously, pondering what might be ailing him. Without hesitation, the bird allowed Lucy to gently lift him into her caring hands.

Upon closer inspection, she discovered that the bird's beak was coated with a sticky substance, possibly from an unfortunate encounter with something he had consumed. Showing remarkable tenderness, Lucy set to work carefully cleaning the beak, alleviating the bird's discomfort for her avian companion. Astonishingly, after the brief act of kindness, the bird regained his vigour and took flight, disappearing into the open sky.

The incident left Lucy in awe of the profound connection between humans and nature. Her willingness to help, and the bird's trust in her, forged a moment of genuine connection amid her tranquil garden. From that day forward, Lucy continued to foster a sanctuary where birds and other creatures could find solace, transforming her garden into a place of harmony and interdependence between all living beings.

CHAPTER SIXTY-THREE

FAMILY CHALLENGES

In the past, Lucy had her own successful business specializing in payroll services. She had numerous private clients and achieved remarkable success. Afterwards, she decided to foster children, but I believe this endeavour was challenging for her as she became emotionally attached to the children.

Lucy's involvement in a community organization aimed at uniting local foster caregivers proved to be a significant chapter in her life. Established to exchange mutual assistance and innovative ideas, this association received sponsorship from the nearby social services agency. It was within the confines of this supportive network that Lucy forged a strong bond with another dedicated foster caregiver named Carole.

The local postman was a part of this group, juggling his role as a postal worker with his commitment to fostering. Having taken in two young girls, aged 15 and 16, he found himself emotionally invested in their lives. Unfortunately, the girls eventually reconnected with their biological mother and opted to return to her care. This decision left the postman great with a profound sense of sorrow and loss.

Lucy's experience, along with the tales of other foster caregivers, illuminated the profound challenges of their roles. The emotional toll of nurturing vulnerable children and adolescents became palpable, highlighting the inherent heartbreak that can accompany such selfless work. The journey of these foster caregivers stands as a testament to the intricate emotions and trials that come with dedicating oneself to this demanding yet deeply rewarding vocation.

Unfortunately, some children take advantage of others' goodwill, which is not their fault, but they possess a keen understanding of how to manipulate people. As the saying goes, the first four years of a child's life are crucial. I recall an incident when Lucy's foster child confided in me while we were alone in the garden. We have a gravel front area leading to steps and a spacious lawn, ending with a large summer house equipped with a table, chairs, and a cooking range. One of the boys they had fostered shared his plans to make changes to the property once he inherited it. He mentioned alterations to various aspects and even spoke about his future after John's passing. I mentioned this conversation to John and asked if he had discussed long-term plans with the lad, but he revealed they hadn't. It's astonishing how the mind of an eight-year-old can contemplate such matters. Despite the complexities, they are still in touch with each other four years later.

Chapter Sixty-Four

A Journey to Self-Worth and Healing

Archie, a foster child, embarked on a transformative path with his new psychiatrist. After approximately a month of sessions, Archie displayed some peculiar behaviours upon returning home. He seemed uncomfortable and preoccupied with his appearance. One day, he provocatively asked his foster mother Lucy, "What would you do if I hit you?" Her response was firm yet compassionate, urging Archie to test the consequences of his actions. Through her interactions, she aimed to convey that healthy relationships were possible, unlike the tumultuous ones he had experienced with his family.

Lucy tried to convey that one day he will have a normal family life and that one day he may get married. Archie expressed his reluctance to get married, believing he didn't deserve

such happiness. Lucy, recognizing the depth of his self-worth issues, empathized
pain. She reassured him, telling him he was valuable and deserving of love. Altho
kept her emotions in check, she silently mourned for him, wishing she could allev.
emotional burdens. She emphasized that everyone holds intrinsic worth and encou
him to envision a future with fulfilling relationships.

During subsequent therapy sessions, Archie gradually disclosed more details about
troubled family background. The psychiatrist considered this openness a positive ste
believing it helped bring repressed issues to light. Archie shared a distressing memory (
being around three years old, hiding behind a settee as his grandfather attacked his niece
Overwhelmed, the psychiatrist urged him to discuss these revelations with his mother,
recognizing the importance of open communication within the family.

As the psychiatrist reviewed Archie's notes with Lucy, his foster parent, she realized that
some aspects of Archie's history had not been previously disclosed to them. She expressed
her belief that they should have been informed earlier. Concerned about Archie's future,
Lucy wondered what would happen when he reached adolescence. Would he be drawn back
to his biological family, driven by the notion that blood ties are unbreakable? Lucy shared
that Archie, currently harbouring intense anger toward his family due to their mistreatment,
often expressed a desire to harm them.

Acknowledging the potential for Archie to reconnect with his family, Lucy and the
psychiatrist discussed their approach. If he decided to re-establish contact and his bond with
his family proved stronger, Lucy resolved to support him. She believed they had provided
him with an opportunity for growth and healing, assuring him that their door would always
remain open, should he need their support in the future.

CHAPTER SIXTY-FIVE

CAROLE'S JOURNEY: FOSTERING AND NAVIGATING A TROUBLED TEEN'S LIFE

C arole, known for her dedication to fostering young children, embarks on a new challenge as she decides to foster an older girl named Lydia. As the story unfolds, Carole encounters unexpected hurdles while trying to provide a stable environment for Lydia.

After two weeks of fostering Lydia, Carole notices a concerning pattern. The girl refuses to attend school and instead sneaks out of the front door, only to re-enter through the back. One fateful day, Lydia returns home drenched, carrying a large rucksack on her

back. Troubled by her appearance, Carole instructs Lydia to take a warm bath v
investigates the contents of the mysterious rucksack.

To her astonishment, Carole finds that the rucksack is missing from Lydia
Suspecting something unusual, Carole cautiously opens the bathroom door and
Lydia bathing a baby lamb. Overwhelmed by the unexpected sight, Carole instruct
to dry herself off and Carole wraps the newborn lamb in a warm towel. Bewildered, C
enquires about the lamb's origin.

Determined to return the lamb to its rightful owner, Carole and her husband emb
on a mission to the five farms in the area. After hours of searching, they finally locate t
distressed owner, a ewe who had been mourning the loss of her baby lamb. The reuni
brings relief to all involved parties.

However, the challenges for Carole and Lydia are far from over. It becomes evident that
Lydia has been engaging in self-harm and making threats to end her own life. The situation
escalates when Lydia climbs to the top of the school roof, posing a serious danger to herself.
In a race against time, Carole calls upon the assistance of the police and social services to
ensure Lydia's safety.

Unfortunately, Carole's frustration mounts when social services fail to promptly address
the incident. Reporting the incident on Monday, Carole received no contact from the authorities by the following Friday, which she deems unacceptable. Carole reflects on the plight
of social workers, who, despite their academic qualifications, lack practical experience in
dealing with individuals like Lydia. Overworked and under-supported, many social workers
eventually resign from their positions.

The situation is exacerbated in Carole's local area, as a private company has taken over
a nearby social services agency due to the high turnover of social workers. This alarming
development highlights the dire need for improved support systems and training within the
social services sector.

Carole's journey as a foster parent to Lydia sheds light on the challenges faced by both the
foster care system and social services. It underscores the importance of adequate support,
training, and timely intervention to ensure the well-being and safety of vulnerable individuals like Lydia.

Chapter Sixty-Six

Health Issues Priorities and New Beginnings

L ucy's current circumstances are marked by health challenges, specifically intense joint pain that can become quite debilitating. On days when the pain is particularly severe, she doesn't hold back in expressing her discomfort. Over the years, she has dealt with significant struggles, though she has noticed some improvement recently, attributing it to the combination of hormone replacement therapy (HRT) and the various medications prescribed for her joint issues. However, her situation took a turn for the worse when she injured her toe, adding insult to her existing injury.

For a considerable period, Lucy had been grappling with a range of health issues, including neck stiffness, fatigue, joint pains, and an unusual rash. Despite the relief HRT brought, she remained concerned about her symptoms. This prompted her to turn to the Internet for insights, leading her to suspect that Lyme disease might be the culprit due to her frequent interactions with her two large dogs during walks. Trusting her instincts, she sought medical help, and after undergoing blood tests, her suspicions were confirmed: she was indeed diagnosed with Lyme disease. Fortunately, her timely diagnosis enabled her to receive appropriate treatment, gradually restoring her well-being.

At the age of 86, Irene is engaged in her battle with Meniere's disease, an intense form of vertigo that induces severe dizziness, disorientation, and bouts of nausea triggered by head movements. This condition forced her to relinquish her driving privileges due to the risk of causing an accident with her limited head mobility. During particularly harsh episodes that lasted days or even longer, she experienced frustration, lethargy, and the fear of being alone and helpless if she were to fall.

Irene's health challenges took on added significance due to her solitary life in Spain. An alarming incident occurred when she had a distressing fall at home, waiting for three hours while crawling to the wall until her neighbour heard her cries and came to her aid. Recognizing the need for change, she made a momentous decision to sell her house and relocate back to the UK to live with her daughter, Lucy, and her husband Ken.

Lucy and Ken's house, with its five bedrooms, four bathrooms, large garden, and driveway, provided ample space for fostering up to four children at a time. However, with their fostering days behind them and the children now leading their own lives, the couple decided it was time to embark on a new chapter.

Considering their recent priorities, Lucy and Ken made the thoughtful decision to downsize to a bungalow in a charming village. This choice would not only provide them with a cosier living space but also offer Irene easier access to entertainment, clubs, and social societies.

During conversations about their move, concerns arose about potential living arrangements during the transition period. Lucy suggested the idea of purchasing a temporary holiday lodge, providing a practical solution while their primary house remains on the market.

Lucy envisioned a new chapter in a village setting, preferably near a village street, where they could easily access amenities and participate in social activities. The prospect of Irene joining a women's group or similar gatherings appealed to her desire for a vibrant community life.

As the couple navigated the complexities of downsizing and the selling process, they held onto hope for a smooth transition. They remained optimistic about finding the perfect bungalow in the charming village that would cater to their evolving needs and aspirations.

Throughout her journey, Irene has remained deeply grateful for the richness of her life. Cherishing memories of a life well-lived, marked by adventures and life's inevitable ups and downs, she found comfort in her belief in something beyond this life. This sense of gratitude and peace carried her through even the most challenging times.

Chapter Sixty-Seven

About the Author

As I conclude Irene's Journey I invite you to delve into my own narrative, that of Lynne Swanson, the author behind these pages. Originating in England and now a resident of Spain, my life's journey has been one defined by diverse ventures and unwavering commitment.

In a prior chapter of my life, I held the mantle of a physiologist, a role that bestowed upon me the privilege of sharing the intricacies of human physiology with countless inquisitive minds. Guiding aspiring Level 3-degree scholars through the labyrinthine process of crafting their theses was a duty I embraced with utmost dedication, propelling them toward the triumphant culmination of their academic pursuits.

Within the controlled confines of laboratories, I wore multiple hats, seamlessly transitioning between orchestrating captivating hands-on sessions that ignited sparks of curiosity and managing the intricate machinery that underpinned scientific inquiry. My tenure at the University of Wolverhampton was marked by scientific exploration, culminating in the publication of a seminal journal article and significant contributions to a spectrum of other published works.

In the year 2003, I embarked on a new odyssey, making Spain my home and carving a niche for myself as an aesthetic practitioner. Fate smiled upon me as I crossed paths with Irene, a serendipitous encounter that would significantly shape the course of my journey. Transitioning into semi-retirement in 2020 provided me with the canvas to paint new experiences.

As I step boldly into uncharted literary terrain, I venture into the realm of book authorship for the very first time. The culmination of this endeavour is the embodiment of Irene's cherished memoirs within these pages. It is my genuine hope that as you traverse these lines, you will find resonance with the narrative I've woven and extract profound enjoyment from the journey I've laid out before you.

Cherished recollections from my early years revolve around the precious moments spent alongside my grandparents in the picturesque village of Port Sunlight. These memories, held dear to my heart, were rekindled in 2008 when Fiona Bruce hosted the Antiques Roadshow in that very village. For those yet to explore its wonders, a visit to this village is an absolute must.

Further details can be found in the link provided below:

https://en.wikipedia.org/wiki/Port_Sunlight#

Leverhulm Memorial

Dell Bridge

Park Street

Lady Lever Art Gallery

Leverhulm Memorial

PHOTOGRAPHY BY
BRIAN SWANSON

REFERENCES

https://en.wikipedia.org/wiki/Blackburn/

https://en.wikipedia.org/wiki/Z-Cars

https://commons.wikimedia.org/w/index.php?curid=5064524

https://www.telegraph.co.uk/cars/classic/patrol-classic-mg-police-car/

https://en.wikipedia.org/wiki/Port_Sunlight

vl

PHOTOGRAPHY BY
BRIAN SWANSON

ABOUT THE AUTHOR

As I conclude Irenes Journey I invite you to delve into my own narrative, that of Lynne Swanson, the author behind these pages. Originating in England and now a resident of Spain, my life's journey has been one defined by diverse ventures and unwavering commitment.

In a prior chapter of my life, I held the mantle of a physiologist, a role that bestowed upon me the privilege of sharing the intricacies of human physiology with countless inquisitive minds. Guiding aspiring Level 3-degree scholars through the labyrinthine process of crafting their theses was a duty I embraced with utmost dedication, propelling them toward the triumphant culmination of their academic pursuits.

Within the controlled confines of laboratories, I wore multiple hats, seamlessly transitioning between orchestrating captivating hands-on sessions that ignited sparks of curiosity, and managing the intricate machinery that underpinned scientific inquiry. My tenure at the University of Wolverhampton was marked by scientific exploration, culminating in the publication of a seminal journal article and significant contributions to a spectrum of other published works.

In the year 2003, I embarked on a new odyssey, making Spain my home and carving a niche for myself as an aesthetic practitioner. Fate smiled upon me as I crossed paths with Irene, a serendipitous encounter that would significantly shape the course of my journey. Transitioning into semi-retirement in 2020 provided me with the canvas to paint new experiences.

Now, as I step boldly into uncharted literary terrain, I venture into the realm of book authorship for the very first time. The culmination of this endeavour is the embodiment of

Irene's cherished memoirs within these pages. It is my genuine hope that as you traverse these lines, you will find resonance with the narrative I've woven and extract profound enjoyment from the journey I've laid out before you.

Printed in Great Britain
by Amazon

28631045R00097